AF454307

English Language Lovers 2

Smiling while Fine-tuning

Cover illustrations by Gabriela Kaziuk and Brian Louzy

Credits for images and quotes not of the authors appear on respective pages.

Canva (https://www.canva.com) assisted with some photographs and insertion of texts.

AI art generators, particularly Microsoft's Bing AI Image Creator, were used for various pictures and illustrations.

Cambridge Dictionary Online helped with the phonetic symbols in pronunciation (https://dictionary.cambridge.org/pronunciation/).

I thank everyone who makes me smile.

The late US author H. Jackson Jr said, "Never make fun of someone who speaks broken English. It means they know another language". That's certainly how I feel. Bilingual and multilingual people are flexible, creative, and open-minded. They make me think and smile, such as this statement from an acquaintance: *"Look at the round and red thing in my bras"*. (The French word "bras" is "arm" in English).

I appreciate the help of non-humans with the artwork and images. For those who have contributed anecdotes and ideas, I hope you will have fun reading your thank you "merci" copy.

I also say "gracias" to those who have promised to buy this book.

Dr Rolade Brizuela Berthier enjoys listening, reading, and storytelling. She lives in France and is a freelance English language teacher in Luxembourg. She has worked in Asia, Australia and Europe for universities, research institutions, government departments, and non-profit organisations. On 23 March 2023, she was a guest speaker at the European Parliament DG Per's anti-racism hybrid event "Why Words Matter". She does an annual pro-bono lecture at Lycée et Collège Hélène Boucher in Thionville, France.

She is the author of "The Whisper of Regrets", a novel about contemporary challenges in relationships, and non-fiction books: "Cross-Cultural Liaison: An Inconvenient Love", "Intelligence, Giftedness: Pre-cradle to Post-grave", "English Language Lovers – Teaching, learning, and conversing before and during the pandemic", and "Clear and Concise Writing".

She has written reports and journal articles on sociological issues, such as ethnicity and crime, employment, migrant women, immigration, and multiculturalism.

Dr Berthier has Master of Social Planning & Development and Doctor of Philosophy (Sociology) degrees from The University of Queensland, Australia. She has a French

Language Certificate from Sorbonne University in Paris and is currently learning Spanish.

She owns www.roladesocietalblog.com, which discusses cultural, political and social issues, and is active on Facebook and LinkedIn.

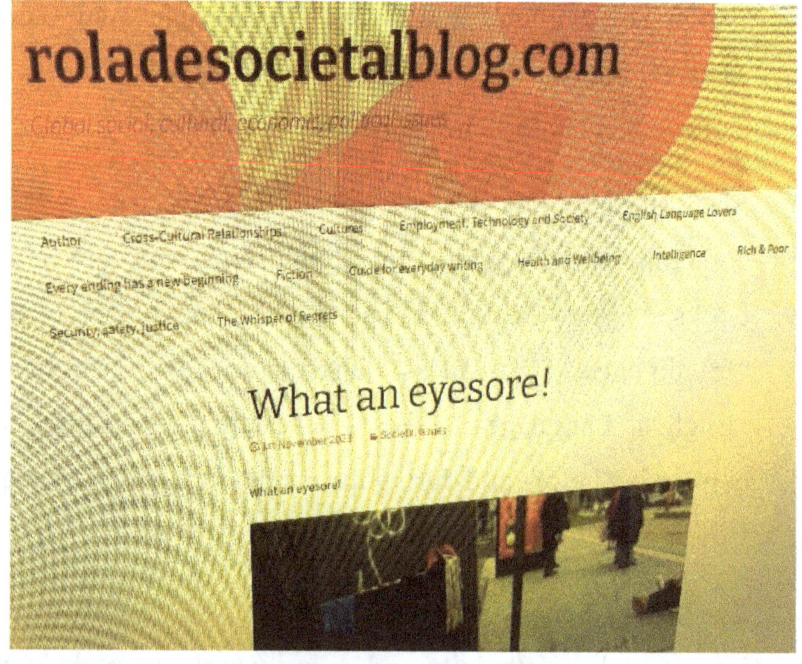

(*His friend has sore eyes with that eyesore.* "Sore eyes" is pain or discomfort in one's eyes; "eyesore" refers to something disagreeable or unpleasant to look at, such as a dilapidated building or dirty and messy environment).

English Language Lovers 2

Smiling while Fine-tuning

By

Rolade Berthier, PhD

Every language has grammar rules. Dictionaries, Apps, and Artificial Intelligence (AI) can help us with our English. However, it is our human touch that makes a difference.

Table of Contents

Never mind the paging; continue reading. There are words for thoughts, thoughts on words, and words to laugh at and make you a better conversant in English. Aphorisms, euphemisms, grammar, jargon, metaphors, similes, tenses, pronunciation, and their friends & relatives await you.

We still need a book like this, even with AI. Why? It is because we are humans, i.e. we learn from each other's experiences, recognise patterns of behaviours and communication styles, think and make decisions, process and retain information, and **laugh.**

As humans, we adapt to changing environments and challenges with consciousness, eagerness, fearfulness, fondness, gladness, kindness, liveliness, mysteriousness, nervousness, playfulness, sadness, sweetness, and other kinds of emotion.

Whereas AI is digital and only mimics human behaviour and thoughts. For example, below is Microsoft Bing Chat*'s response* to my 01/12/23 prompt, **"Give me funny anecdotes and jokes about the English language"**.

Why do we say "an alarm clock" instead of "a clock alarm"? Because if you put the alarm first, it would go off!

Why is it called "after dark" when it's really "after light"?

Why is it that we recite at a play and play at a recital?

Why is it that when we transport something by car, it's called a shipment, but when transport something by ship, it's called cargo?

Why do we park in a driveway and drive on a parkway?

Why is it that when you're driving and looking for an address, you turn down the volume on the radio?"

This is ChatGPT 3.5's response to the same prompt (*US English*) --

"Certainly! The English language, with its peculiarities, irregularities, and nuances,   offers a wealth of material for *humor*. Here are some anecdotes and jokes that play on these aspects:

Homophones and Puns:

Why don't we write with broken pencils? Because it's pointless!

I entered ten puns in a contest to see which would win. No pun in ten did.

Oxymorons and Contradictions:

English can be weird. It can be understood through tough thorough thought, though.

Why is "abbreviation" such a long word?

Spelling Woes:

I'm reading a book on anti-gravity. It's impossible to put down!

The past, present, and future walked into a bar. It was tense.

Idiomatic Expressions:

Never discuss infinity with a mathematician, they can go on about it forever.

I told my wife she should embrace her mistakes. She gave me a hug.

Grammar Gags:

Let's eat, Grandma vs. Let's eat Grandma. Punctuation saves lives.

I'm a big fan of whiteboards. They're re-markable! (sic)

Please note: It's "remarkable" and not "re-markable".

Unlike AI, I had fun writing this book. I woke up in the middle of many nights thinking about my students' stories, hilarious conversations on public transport, and ideas for jokes.

Continue reading to find out my reply to the same request, *"Give me funny anecdotes and jokes about the English language".*

Question: What's the difference between **heaven** and **hell**?

Answer:

In heaven, the Italians are the lovers, the French are the cooks, the Germans are the engineers, the Swiss are the managers, and the British are the police.

In hell, the Swiss are the lovers, the British are the cooks, the Italians are the engineers, the French are the managers, and the Germans are the police.

- *(https://www.englishclub.com/esl-jokes/3-heavenandhell-q.php seen on 28/12/23).*

Spaniard: Where is English less spoken, in heaven or hell?

The English alphabet

- The word "alphabet" comes from the Greek's first and second letters ("alpha" and "beta").
- The alphabet of today's English is a Latin script of 26 letters. It is used by approximately 100 languages and an estimated 2 billion people, making it the most popular language script on Earth.
- The 26 letters of the English alphabet make up 44 distinct sounds (phonemes) with many letters and spelling patterns (graphemes).
- The English alphabet is divided into two major categories – consonants and vowels. When you produce the former's sound, the airflow is wholly or partially cut off. The airflow is unobstructed in the latter when the sound is made.
- Since there are more sounds than letters, some letters have different pronunciations, e.g. "c" is pronounced as /k/ (car) or /s/ (city).
- The most common letter in the English alphabet is "E", and the least used is "Z".
- "Go!" is the shortest grammatically correct sentence in English.
- The two most common words in English are I and you.
- 'Goodbye' came from the 16th-century phrase meaning 'God be with you'.

("God" is capitalised when used at the beginning of a sentence or when referring to a specific, identifiable deity, e.g. Zeus is the god of the sky, and Hera is the goddess of women, marriage and family in ancient Greek religion and mythology. God is not capitalised when it refers to a non-specific deity that goes by another name).

Words Matter

Even with globalisation and digitalisation, the dominant narratives in our society are still favourable to those who are able-bodied, cisgender, Christian, English-speaking, heterosexual, male, wealthy, and White.

International and national laws that aim for justice, dignity, and equity for all have been enacted. However, sometimes, knowingly or unknowingly, we become offensive in our words because of our preconceived thoughts, ideas, and feelings. For instance, I have answered the question *"Where do you come from? You don't sound/look ... "* more than a hundred times, and I expect to encounter the same question at any moment. Do they mean where I was born, where I have studied, worked and lived, where I have immigrated, or where I feel I belong?

A few years ago, the world's media had a ball reporting on the late Queen Elizabeth's Lady-in-Waiting apologising to Fulani, who was repeatedly asked "racially" - loaded questions about her heritage and background at the palace reception. Born in Britain, Fulani claimed on Twitter (now X) that she was asked questions like "What nationality are you?" "Where do you really come from?" "Where do your people come from?" and "What part of Africa are you from?"

It is crucial to listen (and not just hear) what the individuals tell us about their ethnic origins. Ethnicity refers to the identification and belongingness of a person to a group based on cultural distinctiveness expressed in art, family life, food, language, literature, music, religion, ritual, tradition, and national celebrations. Derogatory words due to perceived ethnicity ruin personal, social, and professional relationships. **It's poor communication that no perfect grammar can salvage.**

Written and oral language has power. It can condone, discriminate, embarrass, encourage, harass, inspire, inhibit actions, justify, etc.

Have you heard of master/slave components to describe parts of software and hardware in which one process or device controls another? I have been told that Python, one of the most popular programming languages in the world, eliminated "master/slave" terms in 2018. Kudos to them!

Have you engaged in a conversation in which you said something like, "Our institution has created a blacklist of unreliable providers". We use "blacklist" for something negative or prohibited. In the IT industry, a whitelist comprises elements that are allowed. Doesn't this reinforce notions that black is undesirable while white is desirable? How about using "barredlist"/"blockedlist" and "allowedlist"/"designatedlist" instead?

"Chop Chop!" - This phrase comes from the Cantonese word "kap", which means to hurry up or make haste. Using it sounds like you're making fun of the Pidgin English spoken by Chinese native speakers. Non-offensive phrase – Do it quickly.

Words and phrases matter! This book aims to educate, inform, and entertain. I have made generalisations and used jokes, personal experiences, and observations to emphasise a point and help readers remember correct grammar and essential aspects of the English language.

A

(In UK and US English, "a" is pronounced "eɪ" as in "day".)

Aphorism (UK - ˈæf.ə.rɪ.zəm; US - ˈæf.ɚ.ɪ.zəm)

Aphorisms are one or two sentences that express universal truths; when used in everyday speech, they are known as adages or proverbs. They help us understand and relate the message or directive about life.

Money will buy a dream dog but only kindness will make it wag his tail.

The following aphorisms and adages (or proverbs) are on https://www.yourdictionary.com/articles/examples-aphorisms (accessed on 25 December 2023). I've tweaked them a bit for political correctness and grammatical reasons.

For People:

Actions speak louder than words.

All for one and one for all.

Don't fire until you see the whites of their eyes.

Early to bed and early to rise make a man healthy, wealthy, and wise.

Give people fish, and you feed them for a day; teach them to fish and feed them for a lifetime.

Give them an inch, and they'll take a mile.

Give them enough rope, and they'll hang themselves.

They who fight and run away live to fight another day.

Those who hesitate are lost.

If you lie down with dogs, you wake up with fleas.

Laugh, and the world laughs with you; weep, and you weep alone.

You can fool some of the people all of the time and all of the people some of the time, but you can't fool all of the people all of the time.

You can kill a person, but you can't kill an idea.

You can take the person out of the country, but you can't take the country out of the person.

You made your bed; now lie in it.

You need to take a bull by the horns and a man by his word.

For Life:

A barking dog never bites.

Absence makes the heart grow fonder.

All that glitters isn't gold.

An ounce of prevention is worth a pound of cure.

Children should be seen and not heard.

Doubt is the beginning, not the end, of wisdom.

East or west, home is best.

From the sublime to the ridiculous is but a step.

Genius is one percent inspiration and 99 percent perspiration.

Ignorance of the law is no excuse for breaking it.

Imitation is the sincerest form of flattery.

Possession is nine-tenths of the law.

The more things change, the more they stay the same.

The proof of the pudding is in the eating.

The race isn't always to the swift, nor the fight to the strong, but that's the way to bet.

You can lead a horse to water, but you can't make it drink.

You can't fight city hall.

For Success:

A penny saved is a penny earned.

All things come to those who wait.

Don't hide your light under a bushel.

Don't judge **a book** by **its** cover.

Bear in mind:

Capitalise "judge" before a name when it is the formal title for an individual who presides in a court of law, e.g. Judge Niel Roberts of the Court of Appeal. Use lowercase "judge" as an occupational designation, e.g. Do you know who the judge of the Supreme Court is?

He who pays the piper calls the tune.

If you do what you've always done, you'll get what you've always got.

Know which side your bread is buttered on.

Measure twice, cut once.

****

"Success is not final; failure is not fatal: It is the courage to continue that counts."

- Winston Churchill (1874-1965, Prime Minister of the United Kingdom from 1940 to 1945 and from 1951 to 1955).

****

Australia

(UK - ɒsˈtreɪ.li.ə; US - ɑːˈstreɪl.jə. It sounds
"o·stray·lee·uh").

Austria (UK - ˈɒs.tri.ə; US -ˈɑː.stri.ə)

"If you're having a bad day, just remember that the Salzburg airport has a counter for people who flew to Austria instead of Australia" is a humorous tweet by Melanie Balke in October 2023. However, the airport has confirmed it does not have a desk for absent-minded holidaymakers to Oz who end up in Europe instead (https://www.afr.com/companies/media-and-marketing/austria-or-australia-the-truth-behind-the-viral-internet-meme-20231107-p5ei9z accessed on 20/01/2024).

Meanwhile, this is true:

Tell me **another** joke. Why don't you have *other* jokes? The other<u>s</u> have.

- Another is used as an adjective, which means 'additional' or 'one more' and with a singular noun (e.g. another book, another cook). **(Another + singular noun)**

- It can be used before a plural noun preceded by a number or words/phrases, such as months, a couple of, a few, etc.

  Her mum will moan for another two months.

- Another can also mean 'an alternative' or 'different'.

  This workspace is crowded. Is there another place we can go to?

- Other is an adjective which means 'different' or 'the second of two items' and can be used with singular or plural nouns. **(Other + singular or plural noun)**

  The other person has no reason to audition.

  Those pizzerias are closed at this time. Let's google other places.

- Other can also be a pronoun to refer to things or people; its plural form is others.

  The other driver is (the *other drivers* are) *clever.*

- "Others" is always a pronoun and is not followed by a noun.

I don't want these otters. Aren't there any others?
(others = other otters)

Otters are carnivorous mammals with short ears and noses, elongated bodies, long tails, and soft and dense fur. (Otter is also a term used to describe someone deceitful or treacherous. *I don't have otter friends*).

Otters range from small-clawed to giant ones. They live mainly in freshwater rivers, lakes, and wetlands except in Australia and the Atlantic. The sea and small marine otters are found primarily in the Pacific Ocean.

Unlike this photo, **troupes and troops can have people from different ages, ethnicities, socio-economic backgrounds, and a/gender groups.**

Troupe and troop are homophones, i.e. they sound alike but have different meanings. (*i.e.* = *that is*). The noun troupe refers to a group of theatrical and dance performers. The noun troop refers to a group of soldiers or a collection of people, animals, or things. As a verb, to troop means to move or come together.

The open-air circus will feature a live band with a troupe of international musicians and dancers. There'll be a troop of elephants performing with clowns.

A trouper is a member of an entertainment group, while a trooper is a British cavalry soldier or a member of an American state police.

B

I did my **best** to find the author of the tongue twisters below without any success. Tongue twisters are tricky to pronounce, especially when babbled, but they are entertaining and a fun way to improve pronunciation. So, let's start with these.

Tongue twisters improve pronunciation, diction, and awareness of the sounds of the English language. They can build confidence and are entertaining.

Try saying "She sells seashells at the seashore" slowly, or even repeating them a few times.

A seashore is land bordering the ocean and the sea; a beach is a sandy area along the seashore where people often go to swim, sunbathe, or play.

Baffled? Of course, I'm bewildered by the English language!

We must polish the Polish furniture.

He could lead if he would get the lead out.

The farm was used to produce produce.

The dump was so full that it had to refuse more refuse.

The soldier decided to desert in the desert.

This was an excellent time to present the present.

A bass was painted on the head of the bass drum.

When shot at, the dove dove into the bushes.

(Dove and dived are the correct past tense of dive).

I did not object to the object.

The insurance was invalid for the invalid.

The bandage was wound around the wound.

There was a row among the rowers about how to row.

They were too close to the door to close it.

The buck does funny things when the does are present.

They sent a sewer down to stitch the tear in the sewer line.

To help with planting, the farmer taught his sow to sow.

The wind was too strong to wind the sail.

After several injections, my jaw got number.

Upon seeing the tear in my clothes, I shed a tear.

I had to subject the subject to a series of tests.

How can I intimate this to my most intimate friend?

I read it once and will read it again.

I learned much from this learned treatise.

 I was content to note the content of the message.

The Blessed Virgin blessed her. Blessed her richly.

It's a bit wicked to over-trim a short, wicked candle.

If he is absent, we'll mark him absent.

I incline toward bypassing the incline.

– Anonymous

They've the slimmest chance of participating in this year's Summer Olympics in Paris.

The opposite of fat or slim chance is "most likely" or "good chance".

There's a good chance they'll get a gold medal in race walking.

C

Can ("kæn" or "kən")

Can is one of the modal verbs we use to talk about ability, ask permission, or make requests and offers. The negative form is "cannot"; its contracted version is "can't".

The noun "can" is a sealed container for food and beverages, e.g., cans of beer or soup. It can also mean a receptacle for waste or garbage, e.g. a trash can.

All modal verbs like "can" do not take an 's' for the third person singular, and they use infinitives without 'to'.

He can swim. I can't swim.

Can I open the window?

She can sit next to me. Cannot she?

The past tense of "can" is could.

Other modal verbs:

<u>May and Might</u>

Permission: You may invite your friends.

Possibility: It may rain tomorrow.

Possibility (less likely): She might be exhausted.

<u>Must and Have to</u>

Necessity: Humans must eat and drink. We have to eat and drink every day.

Obligation: You must pay your taxes every year.

Shall (This can only be used with the pronouns "We" and "I").

Future Statement: We shall go there again.

Future Question: Shall I go there again?

Should and Ought to

Responsibility: They should do their weekly assignment.

Suggestion: You ought to ask for your parents' permission.

Will and Would

Future Action: They will come to my birthday party.

Conditional (2nd type – Imagination/Unlikely): I would write a book if I had time.

Conditionals

Conditional sentences express hypothetical or unlikely situations. They can be used in the past, present, or future tense. The auxiliary verbs can/could, will/would, and may/might are used when forming conditionals.

Zero Conditional = If (or "when") + simple present + simple present - this is used for general truths, facts, and everyday occurrences. *When/If the snow melts, the ground becomes icy.*

First conditional = If + will + future tense - this is used to talk about a specific event that is likely to happen. *If there's a transport strike, I'll drive to work.*

(The "if" clause takes a present verb form, and the result clause has "will" + infinitive without to. However, if you are unsure this will happen, we can use the modal verbs "may" or "might". *If it rains, I may/might buy an umbrella*).

If I get promoted, I'll organise a celebration party at home.

If I get promoted, I might organise a celebration party at home.

Also correct: I'll organise a celebration party at home if I get promoted. (There's no comma before "if").

Second conditional = If + past simple tense + would/could/might - this is used to talk about impossible or unlikely conditions in the present or future.

If I won the Euro Million lottery, I would buy a castle in southern France. (This is impossible because I don't buy lottery tickets).

If the verb-to-be is in the "if" clause, use **"were"** and not "was" in the first and second person singular. If I were you, I would parachute and not skydive.

Third conditional

Third conditional = If + past perfect (had + past participle) + present perfect (would/might + have + past participle) - this is used to discuss an imaginary result of something in the past.

She would have attended our annual meeting if she hadn't missed her flight.

(She missed her flight and wasn't at our annual meeting. The result is imagined and can't be changed).

If we had stayed longer in Scandinavia, we would have seen the Northern Lights.

(We didn't stay long enough for the Northern Lights season).

"When once you have tasted flight, you will forever walk the earth with your eyes turned skyward, for there you have been, and there you will always long to return."

– Leonardo DaVinci (1452-1519, painter and engineer).

Chorus of Taylor Swift's song
"Should've Said No" --

You should've said, "No"
You should've gone home
You should've thought twice
'fore you let it all go
You should've known that word
'bout what you did with her
Get back to me (get back to me)

And I should've been there
In the back of your mind
I shouldn't be asking myself, "Why?"
You shouldn't be beggin' for
forgiveness at my feet
You should've said, "No"
Baby, and you might still have me.

3rd conditional - used for
regrets. Swift is talking about
things that happened in the
past and how they could have
been different.

*Taylor Swift, an American singer-songwriter, has won
numerous accolades: Grammy Awards (including four for
Album of the Year - the most won by an artist), Emmy
Awards, and American Music Awards (AMAs).*

D

(UK and US - "d" is pronounced diː)

Divert

(UK - "daɪˈvɜːt" and US - "dɪˈvɜ˞ːt")

While on the tram, my thoughts about work were **diverted** to a teenager's loud voice. She was asking another high schooler a question using a word I had heard for the first time. "Did she Zump him"? I eavesdropped and quickly realised she was referring to her male acquaintance who got dumped on Zoom.

With the search for love globally and online dating, the ending of intimate relationships is likely to occur via videoconference. If someone stops a love affair via Zoom, for example, it can be Zumping (Zoom + dumping; the latter means getting rid of something unwanted). I have heard that some people have also been dumped via Facebook, FaceTime, Skype, Tumbler, and X (former Twitter). Who did the Xumping? She **did** because he **made** her jealous of his many online seductive friends.

Do and Make

"Do" and "make" can be confusing, particularly for those whose first languages have only "make" as a working and assisting verb, such as in French and Italian.

They're deciding where to go.

Do is used when:

a) Performing an action, activity or task, such as doing a crossword/dishwashing/the ironing/the laundry/the washing up.

b) Referring to work that doesn't produce a physical object (do your work/assignment/ housework/job).

c) Talking about your body (do aerobics, do your hair/nails).

d) Speaking about things in general, i.e. to describe an action without saying what the action is, and is used with "something", "nothing", "anything", and "everything".

> *He is up to doing something unprecedented.*

> *She does everything for her employer.*

> *We did not do everything right.*

e) Using these expressions -- do poorly, do business, do a favour, do more harm than good, do your bed, and do your best.

> *He thinks I did well in my presentation.*

Make

We use the verb "make" for constructing, building, or creating something you can touch, e.g., making a dress, making a cup of coffee, and making a meal (breakfast/lunch/dinner).

> *Would you like me to make you a cup of tea?*

> *He always makes breakfast for her.*

We employ "make" in the following expressions --

> make me/her/him/us/them happy

make a choice/comment/complaint/

make decision /difference/mistake

make phone calls/recommendations/suggestions

make an effort/enquiry/an excuse

"Make" collocates with some words related to communication, money, and relationships:

Make the most of it - to use or enjoy something (e.g. holiday, work, relationship) as much as possible.

It is only a one-day training on effective communication, so let's make the most of it.

Make a fortune - make a lot of money

They made a fortune buying and selling used cars.

Make money - make a profit

This NGO made money by auctioning donated goods.

Make a profit - make money

We made a huge profit last year.

Make friends - become someone's friend.

She's good at making friends with people from different cultural backgrounds.

Make fun of someone - mock, tease, or ridicule someone

We shouldn't make fun of someone. She made fun of her colleague.

Make up - to forgive and become friendly again

They made up after a day's row over the briefing paper.

How much do you make?

Enough not to do business on the black market!

The CEO of a large corporation was giving advice to a junior executive. "I was young, married, and out of work," he lectured. "I took the last nickel I had and bought an apple. I polished it and sold it for a dime. The next day I bought two apples, polished them, and sold them for ten cents each."

"I see," said the junior executive. "You kept reinvesting your money and grew a big business." "No," said the CEO. "Then my wife's father died and left me a fortune."

- Reader's Digest (https://www.rd.com/jokes/money/ accessed on 10/02/2024)

E

Euphemisms

They are words or phrases that make offensive, embarrassing, and taboo subjects easier to discuss. They help the speaker avoid being overly blunt and sound polite instead.

Bald is an adjective that describes someone with no hair on their head. It's sometimes confused with bold.

Bold is an adjective describing someone who is brave or something daring.

Pronunciation: UK - bəʊld; US - boʊld.

My neighbour is a gastronome. His spouse has come up with a bold idea to help him stop smoking: no home cooking!

The following are examples of euphemisms (https://examples.yourdictionary.com/examples-of-euphemism.html?msclkid):

<u>Euphemism</u>	<u>The actual word</u>
Death and Dying	
passed away	died
departed	died
gone to heaven	died
gone home	died
passed over to the other side	died
late	deceased
dearly departed	deceased
resting in peace	deceased
no longer with us	deceased

put to sleep — euthanizing a pet

gone over the rainbow bridge — died (for a pet)

States of Employment

letting someone go — firing an employee

between jobs — unemployed

downsised — fired

chose to resign — given no alternative other than to quit or get fired

my position was eliminated — I got fired

taking an early retirement — losing one's job

pursuing other opportunities — quitting or being fired

left the company — quit, walked off the job, or got fired

on a journey of self-discovery — jobless

considering options — unable to find a job

over-employed — a job that is beyond one's capabilities

under-employed — in a job that is below a person's career level

Money and Finance

economical, frugal, cheap	cheap
negative cash flow	in debt
upside-down	owing more on an asset than it is worth
outstanding payment	past-due bill
likes to shop	chronic overspending
economically disadvantaged	poor or impoverished
financially fortunate	spoiled
wealthy, well-off	rich
developing country	economically-poor nation

It's fresh and white. Really? It's <u>cold and snowing</u>.

Euphemism is not synonymous with political correctness.

Political correctness means striving to use words and phrases that are not offensive or discriminatory, particularly to members of different ethnic, gender, socioeconomic, or cultural groups.

Chairman (chair or chairperson)
deaf-mute/deaf-dumb (hard of hearing)
firemen (firefighter)
foreign food (ethnic cuisine)
foreign student (international student)
half-breed/race (multi-ethnic/cultural)
handicapped (people with disabilities or special needs)
mankind (humanity/humankind)
manpower (human resources)
policemen (police officers)
postman (letter carrier)
taxman (tax officer)
tradesman (tradesperson)
uneducated (lacking formal education)

Europe

(UK - jʊə.rəp; US - jʊr.əp)

My Central European student told me about her surprise when her manager, who was born and raised in England, suggested that she attend the professional drafting course. "She often said my write-ups were quite good, so why should I enrol in that course?" she explained. It seemed the former believed it was 'quite good" while the latter meant "a bit disappointing".

It's not only English people who say what they don't mean or their words are misunderstood by others. Depending on the tone and intonation, "very interesting" can mean "impressive" or "nonsense".

Whereas laughter is universal!

How was your walk on the hill?

It was full of ups and downs!

When was this?
In February.

February is not the shortest month of the year. It's May because it has only three letters.

(February, the second month of the year, has 28 days in common years and 29 in leap years when an extra day is added to keep the calendar year synchronised with the astronomical one. February 2024 has 29 days. May is the fifth month of the year with 31 days).

The 2023 edition of the English First (EF) English Proficiency Index analysed the results of the 2022 EF SET English tests of 2.2 million adults from 113 countries. Except for Singapore (2nd) and South Africa (9th), the first 15 countries with "very high proficiency" are members of the European Union (EU). The Netherlands tops the list. (Source - https://www.ef.com/wwen/epi/)

"My objective has always been to get better, no matter where my ranking is".
- Luke Donald

Why do Dutch people have the best English proficiency in the world of non-native English-speaking nations? Their excellence in English is beneficial for global business; likewise, it's also due to international dealing and trading that they are proficient in English.

The African, Arabic, and Chinese speakers might defend their lower EF English Test results compared to the Netherlands by the fact that Dutch is a Germanic language like English. Since they share some roots and characteristics, it is easier for native Dutch speakers to learn and master English.

Kolkman, M (2020) has listed the following English words that came from the Dutch language: anchovy, buoy, caboose, freight, halibut, herring, hoist, keelhaul, skipper, starboard, skate, sledge and sleigh, candy, cookie, crane, gin, knapsack, pen, and pit. According to her, even the dollar came from the Dutch coin "daalder", which the Dutch introduced to the American colonies in the seventeenth century.   (https://www.iamexpat.nl/education/education-news/english-words-you-didnt-know-came-dutch#:~:text=Anchovy accessed on 31/12/2023).

While living Down Under, I heard from a Dutch husband of a Filipino-born Aussie that Australia is a Dutch island sold to the British. I didn't get his joke, so I disagreed with him vehemently. Until now, I haven't progressed much in my Dutch sense of humour, whereas I easily giggle with the American and British playfulness with words.

Https://www.reddit.com/r/learndutch/comments/gxwf0j/a_nederengels_joke/?rdt=53532 (accessed 31/12/2023) invites you to smile or laugh at the following:

"The wife of a Dutch soccer player who playcd in LA (many moons ago) asked her hairdresser for a divorce through the middle of her hair. She wanted to have her hair parted (a.k.a. divided). In the Dutch language, divide and divorce are the same word". - Thunderclogs

"Hahaha, that reminds me of when my boyfriend and I started looking for dogs. I was shocked when I saw 'honden fokkers' on a pretty official website. He couldn't stop laughing when I looked at him with wide eyes and said dog... fuckers?" - CountPenguin

"A dutch lady addressed a group of businessmen in Asia once. She was Home Secretary/minister for interior affairs, just started her first term in office. She told them:
I am the minister for the insides and I'm having my first period". - Rmvandink

Now, on a serious note. At school, I used to say "Holland", and no one ever corrected me. Holland refers to the two provinces in the Netherlands; therefore, it should be the latter if you're talking about the entire country.

"Dutch" is a noun (people - *The Dutch in Luxembourg are resourceful and respectful.*) It can also be an adjective, e.g. *Dutch city, Dutch food*, etc. Wouldn't it be chucklesome if the noun Dutch was Netherlandian (as in Australian) or Netherlandish (as in British)? How about Netherlander?

Let's go Dutch

- Everyone pays for their own bill/expenses.

The idiom "Going Dutch" is recorded as early as 1914 and spread throughout the English-speaking world". It seems to have come from 19th-century Americanism (a Dutch treat or Dutch lunch/supper), which refers to each person paying their own meal. However, the Dutch here are apparently not from the Netherlands but from Germany and Switzerland. (https://www.dictionary.com/e/slang/going-dutch/ accessed on 31/12/2023).

The following disclosures in Edmond Jones' article "Where does the phrase 'Going Dutch' originate?" showcase the instructive and fun nature of Dutch words and phrases in English

(https://www.theguardian.com/notesandqueries/query /0,5753-68084,00.html accessed on 31/12/2023).

"For a more enlightened answer check Brewer's Dictionary of Phrase and Fable but it's something like this. At one point in time or another Britain and Holland weren't too pally and they were the source of derogatory terminology. In the age of chivalry a man paid for the woman's dinner and to 'go Dutch' was to do it how 'they' did it: incorrectly. Double Dutch also derives from the same era, Dutch seeming a strange and convoluted language hence Double Dutch meaning indiscernible, mad and generally all round not on foreign speak". - Dean Holdsworth, Rovereto, Italy

"As far as I know the phrase started with the, successful, British campaign to throw the Catholic, Spanish army out of Protestant Holland. Soldiers having a drink the night before a battle "went Dutch" to avoid being in debt to a colleague if they were killed in the subsequent battle. Similarly, a drink before a battle would also provide a measure of "Dutch courage". - John Dodds, Gifford, UK

"There are many phrases that include the word: 'Dutch', such as Dutch uncle and Dutch courage. They probably entered English at the time of the eastern trade route rivalry. To 'go Dutch' is a contraction of 'In the Dutch fashion', meaning, 'To pay ones share'. Which seems to have been a natural response of traders from a small nation state being patronised by those of a larger neighbour". - Peter Brooke, By Kinmuck, Scotland

"Interestingly in Brussels 'manger à l'hollandaise' or 'manger à la flamande' means the same thing in terms of splitting the bill between everyone present. This may have more to do with the reputation of the Dutch and Flemish being tight with their money (among the French speakers at least) than with the English phrase". - Chris Bourne, Brussels, Belgium

Bear in mind: Idiomatic expressions that mention ethnicity or nationality may cause prejudice or be considered disrespectful.

Singapore finished second in the 2023 EF English Proficiency Index after the Netherlands. This wasn't surprising; although its national language is Malay, English is one of its four official languages (Mandarin Chinese and Tamil are the other two). English is the most widely spoken language in business and by young people. It is the medium of instruction in school, which is based on British English.

Every time I visit Singapore, I'm amazed by their beautiful rhyming Singlish, a colloquial form of English with a distinct accent, ignoring the English grammar.

"Another sign in Singapore translated to 'execution in progress' and we can only hope it was a mistranslation" - Coughland (2023) (https://www.dailymail.co.uk /femail /article-11640975 /Tourists-share-hilarious translated-signs-theyve-spotted-world.html accessed on 22/01/2024).

Here are some slang and Singlish, an indication of localness or *Singaporeanness*, from my friend Bee Sim in Singapore:

Alamak - goodness gracious me! (The literal translation in Malay is somewhat blasphemous- "mother of god")

Atas - snob

Can la! - I can definitely do this.

Can meh? - Can you really do this?

Can wor ... - He said he could do this.

Shiok - The best, nicest thing to do and experience

Kiasu - Fear of missing out ("inbred Sporean culture")

Kiasi - Fear of dying

Back in Europe

While at Walferdange, Luxembourg, on 18 November 2023, two people stopped by my stand before the close of the book fair. One asked me, "Did you write all these books, what's your major?"

"Yes, I did. Which part of the Philippines do you come from?"

"How did you know we're from the Philippines?"

"Physical attributes and the use of 'major'".

"We do look Filipinos. Don't you use the word major in Europe?"

"Here, major isn't an academic discipline or specialisation at the university or college, unlike in the Philippines and the USA".

In the EU, major means considerable, crucial, important, paramount, serious, significant, utmost, or vital. *Shoplifting is a major concern, costing retailers millions of euros every year.* I have never heard someone say, "I can't decide if I should major in English or History". They say, "I'm studying English at the university".

Major is also a military officer rank above a captain and below a lieutenant colonel.

English and Tagalog are the official languages in the Philippines. Filipino English thrived through the introduction of public education taught in English and other instruments of the American colonisation. The influx of Filipino teachers in Japan, South Korea, Thailand, and other Asian countries contributes to the use of US English in this part of the world.

No one owns the English language; it belongs to all.

In our English conversational class about travels to secluded places, a French student asked, "What does 'explore on your own mean'"?

The Lithuanian responded, "It means 'No guide provided or available'".

The Romanian disagreed, "No, it means 'at your own expense'".

I said, "Both answers are correct".

The French continued the conversation. "Explore on your own" sounds exotic. In reality, they want you to spend more money on excursions".

The Spaniard smiled and remarked, "The travel agency just wanted to be positive. It is **easier** to sell a holiday package that way".

The Romanian queried, "Is it 'easier' or 'more easy'"?

That conversation reminded me of a photo I took in a bar in Leiden, The Netherlands, on 30 August 2020, which had a "Think Positive It Makes Life More Easy" sign.

Think positively and **not** think positive.

Think is a verb, so it should be an adverb "positively" and not positive, an adjective. An adjective modifies a noun, e.g. positive thoughts, positive remarks. Thus, "Think Positive" isn't grammatically correct. Yet, it's common to hear English native speakers say this, which shows that the actual usage of language can differ from correct grammar.

We often hear during virtual meetings: "I can hear you loud and clear". I sometimes end my night-time conversations with friends and family with "Sleep tight" and close my emails with "Take care". These phrases have verbs followed by nouns or adjectives and not adverbs. Though grammatically wrong, they sound natural and convey the intended meaning; they are called "flat adverbs".

"More easy" and "Easier"

"More" modifies adjectives with three or more syllables (e.g. more *entertaining, more committed, more accessible*). However, there is no strict grammatical rule against using it for two-syllable adjectives like "easy". Meanwhile, these are the correct comparatives: more boring, more tiring, prettier, sadder (or "more sad").

"Dancing is easier than singing" is more common than
"Dancing is more easy than singing".

Comparative (two subjects - people, events, objects, etc.) and superlative (more than two subjects) adjectives

Add "er" and "est" to one-syllable words to make comparatives and superlatives:

old   older   oldest

young   younger   youngest

If an adjective ends in "e", add "r" or "st":

nice   nicer   nicest

large   larger   largest

If an adjective ends in a vowel and consonant, double the consonant:

f<u>at</u>   fatter   fattest

s<u>ad</u>   sadder   saddest

If an adjective ends in a consonant and "y", change "y" to "i" and add "er" or "est":

merry   merrier   merriest

silly   sillier   silliest

We use "more" to make comparatives and "most" to superlatives for most two-syllable adjectives and those with three or more syllables.

They are more efficient than the QA company.

She is the most reliable employee.

In politics, it seems that the more they change, the more they stay the same.

Farther and further are comparative adjectives and adverbs for "far". *How much farther/further are we swimming?* There is no difference in their meanings; however, using "further" is more common. *We can't swim further; it's too icy.*

There are situations when we cannot use "farther" because it means "additional", "extra", or "higher level". *For further information, please email me at nomail@from.you.*

Farthest and furthest are superlative adverbs and adjectives for "far". "Farthest" is more commonly used with distances (e.g. *It's the farthest we have swum.*), while "furthest" is often found in figurative speech.

F

(UK and US pronunciation of "f" is /ef/, as in fish)

False friends

False friends are words that look or sound similar in two languages but have entirely different meanings. These can be Spanish-English, English-German, Italian-English, or other languages.

The French word "librairie" is a bookstore in English. The French "bibliothèque" is a library in English.

I sang the film 'Mission Impossible' theme song when one of my students presented his excuse for being absent from last week's lesson. *"Sorry, I won't be here next week because I'll be on a mission in Brussels"*. As soon as the laughter subsided, I suggested that they use "business", "business trip", "official trip", or "trip" instead of mission.

They stopped using "mission" for a while but returned to it quickly, as it is such established workplace jargon. They told me there is no other word in their administrative forms for planning and travel reimbursement than "mission".

Having lived and worked in Australia and France, I have heard of and am familiar with many false friends ("faux amis") in English and French languages: here are the common ones:

English	*French*
Actually (really/in fact)	Actuellement (at this moment)
Ancient (former)	Ancien (old but not ancient)
Assist (help)	Assister à (attend but not to help)
Assume (suppose without proof)	Assumer (take on/accept)
Comedian (comic/entertainer)	Comédien/ne (actor who needs not be a comedian)
Editor (finalises writings)	Éditeur (publisher and not editor)

Eventual (endmost)	Éventuel (possible as in "eventuality")
Isolation (segregation/separation)	Isolation (insulation)
Issue (topic/problem)	Issue (exit/ way out)
Journey (travel)	Journée (day)
Library	Librairie (bookstore)
Location (place)	Location (rental/lease/hire)
Realise (understand/notice)	Réaliser (carry out /accomplish)
Raisins (dried grapes)	Raisins (grapes that are not dried)
Resume (start again)	Résumer (summarise)
Sensitive (perceptive)	Sensitive (sensible)
Sympathetic (showing understanding)	Sympathique (nice/friendly)

False Friends in **English and Italian** by Broster, H (2019) (https://dailyitalianwords.com/a-list-of-20-false-friends-in-english-and-italian/):

Accident (English) vs Accidente (Italian)

accident = incidente, infortunio

accidente = coincidence, misfortune, sickness

Argument (English) vs Argomento (Italian)

argument = discussione, litigio

argomento = topic, subject, theme, evidence

Here are other examples: "Korista ruum (clean up the room) in Estonian and korista ruumis (decorate the dead body) in Finnish. Also, if Estonian orders piim (milk) in Finland he will get piimä (sour milk). Milk in Finnish is maito". – Vladraptor (https://www.reddit.com/r/Ask Europe/ com ments/k8xdfd/false_friends_of_a_translator_what_are_the/ accessed on 18/01/24).

"I believe that Polish and Czech translators must have a lot of fun while translating PL-CZ or CZ-PL. There are a ton of false friends between our languages which sound either funny or so close to the source language but mean a total opposite. For example, in Polish czerstwy means stale, but in Czech čerstvy means fresh. Or zachód means 'west' while in Czech it means 'a toilet'". - Mahwan (https://www.reddit.com/r/AskEurope/ comments/k8xdfd/falsefriends_of_a_translator_ what_are_the / ?rdt=50239 accessed on 18/01/24).

There's plenty of fish in the lakes of Slovenia.

"Plenty of fish in the sea/ocean/lake" is not a false friend but an idiomatic expression meaning there are many other people you can have relationships with. *You should assure your son that there's plenty more fish in the sea.*

(In UK and US English, the letter "g" is pronounced /dʒiː/).

Grammar

(UK -ˈgræm.ər; US -ˈgræm.ɚ)

Grammar is a set of rules that dictates how a language works, making communication easy. It is hard to speak and write in English without knowing its grammar. Often, native English speakers do not intentionally study grammar to be effective communicators, as they learn this by hearing from their family, friends, and the environment they were born and raised. Meanwhile, learning a language later in life usually involves more formal or direct study or instruction.

The word grammar came from the Greek grammatikē technē, which means "art of letters". In linguistics, grammar also refers to studying structural rules, including morphology, syntax, phonetics, semantics, phonology, and phonetics.

Grammar showcases the linguistic behaviour of groups of people (Australian, American, British, Canadian, Dutch, Indian, Singaporean, etc.) rather than individuals, as shown in their idiomatic expressions and slang. However, there is grammar shared by all or most native and non-native English speakers, e.g. In simple sentences, there is subject - verb - object word order (Sidney plays the guitar.) and consistency in tenses (She *said* they *had done* it. Past perfect tense: had + past participle - the "doing" happened before the "saying").

In 2023, around 1.5 billion people (18%) worldwide spoke English natively or as a second language (Dyvik, 2023). Whether it is or is not the language we use at home, we can continue to improve how we use it. There's always room for improvement.

Understanding how grammar works is fundamental for all users, as it helps make them more effective communicators in writing and speaking. Knowledge of grammar enables you to combine words into coherent sentences and form the latter into paragraphs that convey what you want to say without confusion or misunderstanding.

Grammar includes the rules of spelling and punctuation. With online language applications and software, spelling has become a non-issue; a difficulty may arise when these IT gadgets are out of your reach when you are asked to write on a flirt chart or smart board. On the other hand, the role of punctuation should never be underestimated, as when correctly used, it can clarify the meaning of your sentences.

"Your grammar is a reflection of your image. Good or bad, you have made an impression. And like all impressions, you are in total control". - Jeffrey Gitomer (https://www.brainyquote. com/topics/grammar-quotes accessed on 03/01/2024)

"Like everything metaphysical, the harmony between thought and reality is to be found in the grammar of the language". - Ludwig Wittgenste (https://www.brainyquote. com/topics /grammar-quotesaccessed on 03/01/2024)

"Grammar is a piano I play by ear. All I know about grammar is its power". - Joan Didion (https://www.brainyquote .com/topics/grammar-quotesaccessed on 03/01/2024)

Reader's Digest (https://www.rd.com/list/grammar-jokes/ accessed 03/01/2024):

*Q: Why should you never date **apostrophes**? A: <u>They're</u> too **possessive**.*

An apostrophe (') has two functions: it indicates possession (The obsession of Orly = Orly's obsession), and it is used to replace letters that have been omitted, as in contractions (e.g. They have bought an electric car. = They've purchased an electric vehicle).

In singular form, possession is marked by **'s**, written immediately after the possessor (Sam's SUV is parked outside). In a plural sentence that ends in **s**, the apostrophe is after the **s** (The Jones' house is near the Protestant church).

The verb "possess" means to own or control a person, animal, object, or property. *They possess a vast agricultural land in Peru.*

The adjective "possessive" means clinging to someone or something, as in "mine". *Her partner is highly possessive; he doesn't allow her to grocery shop alone.*

Magic Mirror on the Wall, Who is the Funniest one of all?

Photo courtesy of Bing

As of today, possession of mirrors will be outlawed.

This decision comes after a lot of reflection. - https://upjoke.com/possess-jokes

(Reflection is a deeper form of thinking or learning. It can also mean the production of an image by a mirror).

Genuine

(Genuine is pronounced "'dʒen.ju.ɪn" in UK and US English).

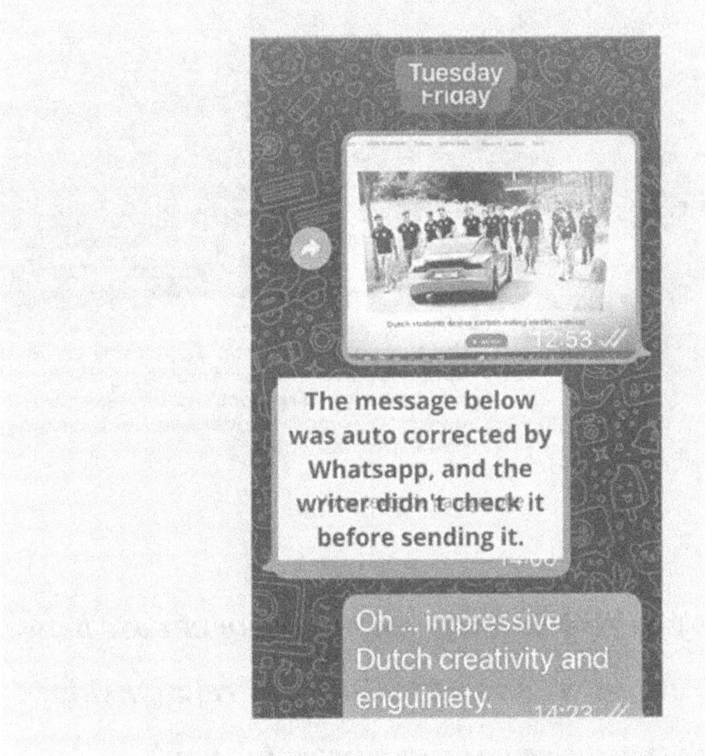

The sender wanted to write in·genu·ity (ɪndʒɪˈnjuːɪti),

meaning original, inventive and intelligent. Enguiniety is not an actual word; however, the adjective enguine can be the opposite of "genuine" (original, authentic – adjective; genuinely – adverb).

"If you're genuinely asking me to choose between my career as a reporter and our relationship; well then, I've got some news for you".

\-   https://upjoke.com/genuine-jokes seen on 28/12/23

H

(UK and US - "h" /eɪtʃ/)

Homographs are words with the same spelling but different meanings, e.g. park is a public play area (noun), or (verb) to bring a vehicle to a stop and leave it there temporarily.

Abstract:

- an idea or existing only in thought
- a summary of a scientific article, document, or any text

Abuse:

- to use (something) for a wrong purpose

- to treat (a person or an animal) with cruelty or violence regularly or repeatedly

Address:

- the particular place where someone lives or an organisation is located
- a formal speech delivered to an audience

... The rest is on your hand.

Homophones are words with the same pronunciation but different meanings and may or may not have the same spelling; for instance, there/their/they're.

air   heir

aisle   isle

ante-   anti-

eye   I

... The rest is on your hand.

Homonyms have the same spelling and pronunciation but have different meanings, e.g. right means correct or the opposite of left.

Bank - a financial institution where you can deposit or withdraw money or the side of a river.

Bat - a flying nocturnal mammal that lives in a cave or a piece of sports equipment used to hit a ball.

Bow - a knot tied with a ribbon (or as in "bow-tie") or a weapon used to shoot arrows (bow and arrow).

... The rest is on your hand.

He drinks his drinks non-stop, getting drunk as a boiled owl. (He's thoroughly drunk).

Hyperbole

Hyperbole has three syllables and is pronounced haɪˈpɜːbəli (hai.puh.bulee).

Hyperbole (noun) is an exaggerated or overstated comparison that should not be taken seriously. It came from the Greek hyper "beyond" and bole "to throw" and is used to emphasise or obtain a literary effect.

My feet are killing me.

Hyperbolic (adjective) means an excessive or overdramatised claim.

I enjoy listening to her hyperbolic statements.

I

Idioms and Idiomatic Expressions

An idiom is a word or phrase with a figurative meaning, i.e. it cannot be understood literally. It comes from the Greek word "idios", which means distinct, personal, or private. So, I believe it originally meant a speech peculiar to a group of people or country.

Idioms spice and make speech or writing more memorable. They're derived from historical events and popular culture, such as books, films, shows, and songs. For example, the idiomatic expression "head over heels" (meaning "in love") is from the 1998 movie "Meet Joe Black" starring Claire Forlani, Brad Pitt, and Anthony Hopkins. *"Fall head over*

heels. I say find someone you can love like crazy and who will love you the same way back". Since then, I've heard "head over heels" in other films, including in the Netflix series "Griselda", a fiction inspired by real events about Griselda Blanco's "The Godmother" rise from Medellín to Miami's drug empire.

Idioms and idiomatic expressions are important in everyday written and spoken English. Their structures have no formula and don't always make sense when taken word by word. Therefore, one has to know their meaning and usage by heart. They are the hardest phrases to translate and interpret.

Idiom	Meaning
A blessing in disguise	A good thing that seemed terrible at first
Beat around the bush	Not speaking directly or precisely
Better late than never	Better to do it late than not at all
Bite the bullet	Face a difficult situation bravely
Break a leg	Good luck
Call it a day	Stop working on something
It costs an arm and a leg	Very expensive

Cut corners	Do something poorly to save time or money
Give someone the benefit of the doubt	Trust what the person says
Go back to the drawing board	Start all over again
Hang in there	Don't give up or surrender
Hit the nail on the head	Say or do something exactly right
Hold your horses	Be patient or wait
It's the last straw	Patience has run out
It's not rocket science	It's not complicated
Kill two birds with one stone	Achieve two goals with a single action
Make a long story short	Say it briefly
Miss the boat	It's too late
No pain, no gain	No miracle; work hard for what you want
Piece of cake	Something very easy to do
Pull someone's leg	To joke with or tease someone

The lemon is worth the squeeze.

Origin: Squeezing oranges to make juice is labour intensive. Hence, the expression means the outcome justifies the effort put into it.

Spill the beans	Reveal a secret or confidential information
The best of both worlds	It's an ideal situation
Under the weather	Sick or unwell
Your guess is as good as mine	I don't have a clue, or I have no idea

Idioms and idiomatic phrases aren't easy to translate

"**I** don't know what's « les bons comptes font les bons amis » in English. Do you know? "

"**I** think 'Les bons comptes font les bons amis means that when you owe your friends money, you've to pay them back as soon as possible; otherwise, it can ruin your friendship. Hence, a similar idiomatic expression in English is 'A debt paid is a friend kept'".

It literally means:

Les bons comptes→ Good accounts

font → make

les bons amis → good friends

According to this proverb, each must pay their respective debts to maintain the friendship. As such, this is similar to these English proverbs: "Short reckonings make long friends" and "A debt paid is a friend kept".

If you borrow money from a friend, you should return it as soon as possible. When you owe your friends money and don't pay it or take a lot of time to do it, they might say, "Les bons comptes font les bons amis" as a reminder that your friendship might not last long unless the situation changes soon.

If you owe a friend money, you can say: "Je vais te rembourser dès que possible, les bons comptes font les bons amis". This means "I will pay you as soon as possible; I value our friendship, so I will do my best to honour my debt".

In times of need, it's better to have friends than money.

"Giving a due" means praising someone or people for something good they have done. It also refers to recognising those who deserve it even though you might dislike other things about them.

India

India and China are the two most populous countries in 2023. According to the UN DESA Policy Brief No. 153, they will remain in their positions in 2050 with projected populations of 1.670 billion and 1.313 billion, respectively (https://www.un.org/development/desa/dpad/publication/un-desa-policy-brief-no-153-india-overtakes-china-as-the-worlds-most-populous-country/ accessed on 30/12/2023).

Let's put aside the silver medallist and focus on the gold winner.

English is India's official government language. More Indians speak English than Australian, New Zealander and British citizens combined. Due to their country's colonial history, Indians use British English mixed with home-grown words and flaws.

My Indian-born Australian friend has told me that India is divided by ethnicities but united by the English language.

Dr Sridhar has revealed the following Indian English words and phrases (Renardsworld.wordpress.com/2020/04/14/15-funny-common-phrases-of-indian-english-you-are-unaware-of/ accessed 30/12/2023), some of which I have also heard and misunderstood.

"Out of Station

My friend, to be on the safe side, I am informing you in advance regarding my inability to attend your function since I am out of station. As if the person is waiting outside the railway station indefinitely and is sort of holding a secret. Why can't you simply say 'I am not here' or 'I am in so and so city'?

Slowly Slowly

A Husband is talking to his wife about their one year old child… 'Slowly slowly he will start talking & walking, or I slowly slowly adopted the environment in the factory'. Just say 'slowly' once; that is enough.

Passing Out Of The College

'I passed out of my college', meaning I completed graduation. In the UK, USA, Australia or

New Zeland 'Graduation' or 'Convocation' is used. One graduates from the college and not passes out. 'Passed out' is used if somebody drank alcohol heavily and is unconscious.

Don't Eat My Brains

This one is used when somebody is under stress and is used during times of irritation; just yelling to the other person 'Stop bugging me!'

Expired

It's common for people to refer death this way. Example – My dad expired. The term 'expired' is used for products that come with expiry dates. Instead one can say 'My dad passed away'.

Using 'No' in a question

Commonly, every question is followed by the word, 'No'. 'You are going to Delhi no?' or 'Are you going to bed no?' It should be, 'You are going to Delhi, aren't you?'

Mother Promise/God Promise

It's common to hear these sentences… When somebody says…. *'Mother promise I didn't do it'* or *'God promise I did it'*… it simply means you don't have any choice but to believe that person. One is aware of Mother's promise or God's promise but not Mother promise or God *Promise.*

The word 'promise' is mentioned in Oxford Dictionary but not 'mother promise'/'God Promise.' 'Mother promise' is literally the English translation of the Hindi sentence, 'Ma Kasam.' There is no need to drag your mother or God into the discussions.

Timepass

Again, this term not found in dictionary. It is an expression used to kill the time. You can think of it as, 'I am passing the time'.

Paining

It's commonly used during conversations. *'My head is paining,'* or *'My body is paining'*, which replaces the word 'Hurting'". (*sic*)

Sic - pronounced "sik" - is a Latin word meaning "thus" (so) and is used in English as an adverb to indicate that the text or speech is the reproduction of the original. It is italicised and placed inside brackets after a word or phrase that the writer thinks to be incorrect but is intentional. I have added (sic) in the above-quoted text because there are errors relating to grammar, choice of words, and sentence structure. For example, "I am in so and so city" (sic). I am in a so-and-so city.

YADAV (2018) makes us smile at these billboards:

The adjective facial (face – noun) and the verb dye (to change colour) seem to have been spelt how the local inhabitants pronounce them.

As far as I knew, "baggar" didn't exist in English. Still, I checked it online and found that Baggar (or Bagar) is a town in Rajasthan, India.

A beggar is a person who lives by asking people for money. Beggars are often homeless or have no fixed abode (home); they "sleep rough". *It will become a city of beggars <u>within</u> three years.*

J

("J" is pronounced "dʒeɪ" in UK and US English, as in jump.)

Jargon

(UK - ˈdʒɑː.gən; US - ˈdʒɑːr.gən)

Jargon is a special word and phrase used by particular groups of people, especially in their occupation or by specialists, which are unfathomable to outsiders (e.g. golden parachute – a corporation's term for a generous departure package).

Avoid jargon when communicating with people of mixed backgrounds and not from the same organisation or group. For instance, you may suggest to your colleague, "We need to have a helicopter view of the situation," which means "an overview or general survey of the situation". However, this may be confusing or incomprehensible to artists.

Slang is not jargon.

Slang refers to words or phrases not widely recognised or accepted in Standard English but used by specific groups. Australian slang, which often ends in "o", "ie/ies", or "y", is entertaining. For instance, Aussies call their barbecue "barbie", which the Americans and the British do not. The use of slang is more informal than colloquialisms and can sometimes be vulgar, e.g. buzz off (go away) and suck (annoying or disgusting).

Colloquial language is widely accepted and used mostly in everyday informal verbal conversation. They reflect the speech of particular eras, dialects, and regions, e.g. *I ain't in the mood for dancing* (US). *When are you **gonna** visit me?* (The US's gifts to the world via its Hollywood; ain't = am not, gonna = going to).

In July 2022, my sister and brother-in-law from OS (slang for Australia), visited us. When we picked them up at Luxembourg airport, they were surprised to see the word "rooted" in front of the building for everyone to see.

Brother-in-law to me: Look, look! Isn't that vulgar?
Me: That's European English. They don't mean "screwed".
Brother-in-law: It's an Aussie slang for "having sex".
Me: "Support" for those outside Down Under. Let's "root for" Les Blues.

K

(UK and US - keɪ)

Knowledge

(UK and US pronunciation - ˈnɒl.ɪdʒ)

Knowledge (noun) – is an awareness of facts and situations, a familiarity with individuals and organisations, or having practical skills to circumnavigate challenges.

> *She has knowledge about the new taxation legislation.*

To know (verb) - to realise or to be aware of something through observation, enquiry, or information.

> *She knows the new taxation legislation.*

> *I need to know how to escape from paying the carbon tax.*

Knowledgeable (adjective) - proficient, well-informed, well-versed

> *Since she's knowledgeable about it, I should see her at once.*

Unknowledgeable (adjective) – ignorant, unfamiliar

> *I'm unknowledgeable about taxes.*

Knowledgeably (adverb) – describes a verb or adjective that suggests knowledge or know-how.

> *She will do it knowledgeably, and you'll receive a tax rebate.*

Knowledge gives confidence and can bring positive changes to individuals and societies. Likewise, it can destroy living and non-living things if it is in the hands of evil people. Its impact on thoughts and actions might not be so noticeable, but it never fades away.

Knowledge vs Wisdom

Knowledge is gained through formal education or self-study by reading books, researching, analysing, and thinking. Wisdom (noun) is a state of being wise (adjective - having the ability to make sound judgements based on a thorough understanding and extensive life experience). Wisdom is built upon knowledge, yet you can be knowledgeable about a particular subject but be unwise. The late Nelson Mandela was knowledgeable and wise. He was familiar with the political complexity in South Africa and was prudent and sensible in his judgement and political decisions.

Though we often put salt in our avocados and eat them with vegetables, they are biologically fruits because they contain seeds and grow from flowering plants' ovaries. In Asia, they eat avocados as dessert, mixing it with sugar and milk. Knowledge about avocados' versatility gives you choices. Eating avocado smoothie instead of cakes and sugary soft drinks as snacks is wisdom.

Beware of false knowledge; it is more dangerous than ignorance.

George Bernard Shaw George Bernard Shaw (1856-1950, Irish playwright)

The subject of wisdom will be discussed again later.

L

(UK and US - el)

Latin

(UK and US pronunciation - ˈlæt.ɪn)

British vs American
Conversation

Latin Words and Influence on the English Language

It has been estimated that 60% of the English words originated from Latin. Here are some of them:

English	Latin	Meaning
agenda	agere	a list of items

		to be discussed during a meeting
compulsory	compulsorius	mandatory, obligatory
deceptive	deceptivus	misleading
delete	deletus	erase (Latin "erasus"), remove
fluent	fluentem	well-versed, eloquent
gown	gunna	long dress
horrid	horridus	terrible, awful
(to) ignite	ignire	light, kindle
nefarious	nefarius	vicious, wicked
omen/ominous	omen/ominosus	sign/fateful
opposite	appositus	contradiction, facing something /someone
refund	refundere	repay, give back
scholar	scholaris	intellectual, learned person
Ultimatum	ultimus	final

veto	veto	forbid, stop the process of a decision
via	via	by way of
vintage	vindemia	antique, retro

De facto, which sounds like "day FAK-toh" or "dee fakto", is a Latin word meaning "in fact". It describes an actual situation or practice irrespective of whether it is officially recognised by legislation or other legal norms and standards.

While on a bus from France to Luxembourg, I heard a man in his security guard uniform telling the person sitting behind me about his de facto wife's (or "de facto spouse") constant criticism about his outfit choice and mundane decisions.

It's not made in heaven but on earth.
De facto doesn't exist there; you've to be married.

You must be joking!/kidding!

In Australia, a de facto relationship is defined in Section 4AA of the Family Law Act 1975; i.e. you and your former partner, who may be of the same or opposite sex, have a "relationship as a couple living together on a genuine domestic basis". However, it is not a de facto relationship "if you are legally married to one another or if family relates to you". The Federal Circuit and Family Court of Australia (known as the Court) deals with issues related to the children and financial disputes of de facto relationships like those of married couples. (Commonwealth Courts Portal Federal, Circuit and Family Court of Australia. Family Law https://www.fcfcoa. gov.au/fl/pubs/defacto#:~:text).

Non-Latin: licking, liking, leaking

Licking - lɪk.ɪŋ (Moving the tongue across the surface of someone or something.

Licking is dog's natural behaviour. Your dog licks you to get your attention, demonstrate bonding, express love, and groom itself.

Liking - laɪ.kɪŋ (Feeling of fondness, appreciation, or approval).

Liking the Australian lifestyle is hating littering in public places.

Littering, which is throwing any waste object on the ground instead of putting it in trash cans or garbage bins, is an offence in some countries.

Litter is any waste, rubbish, or trash that hasn't been disposed of properly.

There's litter in parks, residential buildings, roads, bus stops, and train stations. Examples of this litter are candy wrappers, cigarette butts, papers, plastic bottles, and leftovers.

Leaking - liːkɪŋ (Losing or admitting contents, e.g. liquid or gas, through a hole or crack).

"A**dv**anced thanking" sounds weird. These are the correct phrases:

Thank you

I appreciate your help

Thanks for your attention

"Thanks in advance" is presumptuous and may put the recipients in an awkward position if their answer is "no".

M

(UK /US - em)

Methapor

(UK and US - ˈmet.ə.fɔːr)

A metaphor is a figure of speech that describes an action, object, person, or situation in a literally untrue way but helps explain an idea. *Robert has a heart of gold, which* means he is generous. If you take this literally, it sounds weird or without any sense, as no one's natural heart is made of a soft, yellow, metallic chemical element.

Metaphor adds colour to one's speech; it's often found in literature and poetry.

Common metaphors used in everyday life from https://www.thelifevirtue.com/metaphors-about-life/ (accessed on 25/12/2023). I have tweaked them a bit for clarity.

He is an old flame I used to date.

Time is money.

Life is a race you keep on running.

His lawyer is a shark.

She got cold feet and left.

I was quickly left in the dust.

Life is a battle; you have to fight and struggle to win.

He is the light of my life.

My daughter is the apple of my eye.

My room has become my prison.

Life is a journey; sometimes, the roads are straight and sometimes winding.

You have aged like a fine wine!

Life is a rose; you get the thorns with the flower.

Laughter is the best medicine.

My heart's a stereo, and it beats for you!

Go for a walk before you become a couch potato.

My life is a roller-coaster, with all its ups and downs.

I am happy as a clam.

This is a stepping stone for success.

She has a heart of stone.

After being arrested, he turned into a rat.

My computer is a dinosaur.

The class turned into a zoo when the substitute showed up.

She was fit as a fiddle!

This job is the winning lottery ticket.

Life is a puzzle; you can only see the picture when you put all the pieces together.

Stop beating a dead horse.

He was a diamond in the rough.

The world is your oyster.

Life is an ocean. "Sometimes it calms seas, and everything is smooth sailing. Other times you have to face strong waves or swim against a current".

A Chinese spouse said to her Australian wife, **"I don't like it when you use Aussie slang and metaphor. My blood boils when you do that"**.

Blood boils is a metaphor, meaning *it causes anger*

– I'm angry when you do that.

Like metaphors, similes directly compare two people, things, or situations. Unlike the former, the latter use "like" or "as".

*I don't believe that he sleeps **like** a baby.   She is **as** intelligent **as** you.*

Simile

Pronunciation: sɪm.ɹ.li (UK); sɪm.ə.li (US)

A simile is a figure of speech used to make a description more emphatic or vivid.

My sister-in-law dreamt (also correct -- dreamed) that she sang "Touch Me in the Morning" **as** melodic **as** Diana Ross. She woke up **like** a superstar.

Valentine's Day is **as** important **as** Halloween. So, for our next get-together, will February March? Unfortunately not, but April May.

(Will February **march**? Unfortunately not, but April **may** work).

"Life is **like** a camera. Focus on what's important. Capture the good times. And if things don't work out, just take another shot".

- Ziad K. Abdelnour (https://www.azquotes.com /quote/810768?ref=life-is-like accessed on 04/01/2024)

N

Noun and its Relatives

(noun - naʊn)

A simple sentence is an independent clause with only one idea. It is composed of a **noun** -subject (doer of the action), a verb (the action or state), descriptors (adverbs and adjectives), and sometimes an object (receiver of the action).

They climbed the peak of Mt. Everest quickly. (They - subject; climbed - verb; the peak - adjective; Mt. Everest - object; quickly - adverb).

A compound sentence consists of two independent, related clauses.

Example: *They climbed the peak of Mt. Everest,* and *their colleagues congratulated them.*

A complex sentence has one independent clause and one or more dependent clauses (also known as "subordinate clause" because it cannot stand alone).

Example: *They climbed the peak of Mt. Everest even though they were already in their 60s.*

Nouns

Nouns are subjects, i.e. names of people, places, things, ideas and animals. **Peter** is my son's best friend.

Pronouns

Subject pronouns take the place of nouns and are used as subjects: I, you, he, she, it, we, you, and they.

Example: **They** will help us distribute the leaflets.

Object pronouns are used as direct objects, indirect objects or objects of the preposition: me, you, him, her, it, us, you, and them.

Example: Would you please give **her** my phone number?

Possessive pronouns act like adjectives and show possession: my, your, his, her, its, our, your and their.

Example: The young mothers are breastfeeding **their** babies.

Also: mine, yours, his, hers, its, ours, and theirs. Example: It is my car = It is **mine**.

Use an object pronoun after a preposition; e.g. I love mangoes more **than** (or 'as') him = I compare him with mangoes. Use subject pronoun after conjunction (e.g. I love mangoes more than he does) = I compare myself with him.

Verbs

Verbs express action or link the subject and the predicate (object, adjective, and adverb).

*Lucy **does** her assignments every day.*

Adjectives

Adjectives modify nouns and pronouns; they are placed before the noun or pronoun.

*The new government building has a **wooden** door.*

Adverbs (again, almost, always, ever, frequently, generally, hardly ever, nearly, nearly always, never, occasionally, often, rarely, seldom, sometimes, twice, usually, and weekly)

Adverbs modify verbs, adverbs and adjectives, usually ending in **ly**. *The football players are entering **quietly** and **slowly**.*

It is relatively easy when the sentence has only one verb, as the adverb usually goes before the verb. *I almost made it. I always go to the cinema.*

My students, however, are often uncertain when placing adverbs in a sentence with two verbs, e.g. I *am (always) working* hard.

Adverbs always follow **the verb to be** (am, is, are, was and were). *I **am** <u>sometimes</u> angry at him. They **were** <u>never</u> late with deliveries.*

When two or more words form the verb (e.g. can climb), the adverb is after the first verb. *She **has** <u>almost</u> made it to the championship.*

The adverbs "always," "also", and "probably" go with a verb, and they are found in the middle of the sentence. *George probably commutes by train.*

Adverbs "all" and "both" come before an adjective or verb. *They are both efficient. They all wanted a pay raise.*

For more than two or more adverbs at the end of the sentence, the adverb of **manner** comes first, then **place** and **time**. *He spilled <u>badly</u> the paint <u>on the new floor</u> <u>yesterday</u>.* (also correct - spilt)

Conjunctions

<u>Coordinating conjunctions</u> join words, phrases and clauses of equal grammatical rank in a sentence (and, but, for, nor, or, yet, and so).

*My students **and** I managed to get there on time.*

You can start your sentence with a coordinating conjunction to emphasise but do this sparingly and only with semi-formal and informal correspondence.

<u>Correlative conjunctions</u> are pairs of conjunctions used together to make a connected sentence (e.g. either/or, neither/nor, not only/but, whether/or).

Not only do I enjoy writing, but I also love reading.

<u>Subordinating conjunctions</u> join independent and dependent clauses to show a cause-and-effect relationship, a contrast, or other kinds of connection between the clauses. These are: after, although/though, as, as if, as long as, as much as, as soon as, as though, because, before, by the time, even if, even though, even when, if, so that, in case, in the event of/that, now that, once, only, only if, provided that, since, so, supposing, that, till/until, unless, when, whenever, where, whereas, wherever, whether or not, and while.

Although I do not like her, I will attend her farewell party.

You may start a sentence with a subordinating conjunction if the dependent clause comes before the independent clause (e.g. Unless he comes with me, I am not going there).

The noun « notice »

The Australian authority thanks you for noticing this *notice* on crocodiles. Failure to notice this *notice* will not lead to political persecution but prosecution. ("Notice" is also a regular verb).

We should avoid redundancy when communicating unless it is for emphasis. This is a better version: *Failure to follow these instructions may result in prosecution.* Prosecution is a legal action to redress or punish a violation of law or crime committed. Persecution is harassment designed to injure or cause someone or a group of people to suffer because of their beliefs, lifestyle, etc.

'In German, 'Australien' means Australia and 'Australisch' is Australian. Doesn't this make sense: 'Australisch' - the noun (Australia) - and Australien - the adjective (Australian)?

Yes, but

"Common sense, to most people, is nothing more than their own opinions".

- William Hazlitt (1778-1830, English essayist and philosopher).

O

(UK - əʊ, US - oʊ)

Oxymoron

(ɒk.sɪˈmɔː.rɒn - UK ; ɑːk.sɪˈmɔːr.ɑːn - US)

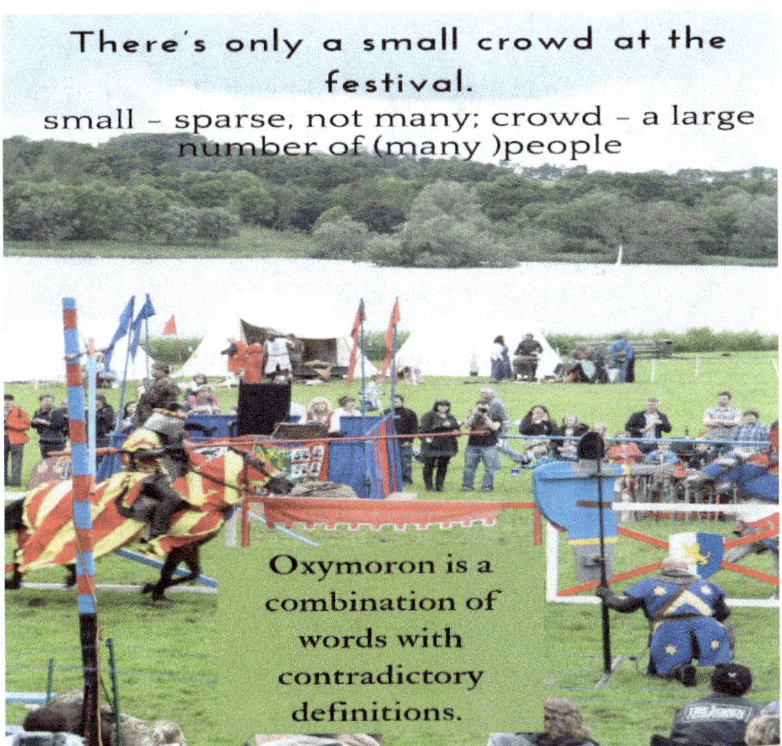

Oxymoron came from the Greek words "oxus" (sharp) and "moros" (dull). "Sharply dull" is an oxymoron itself. (Sharply - an adverb - is needed before the adjective "dull"). Its plural forms are oxymora and oxymorons.

Examples of oxymorons:

Act naturally – Why didn't the children act naturally? (To act - to perform or behave unexpectedly or unnaturally to achieve a desired outcome. "Naturally" refers to an absence of pretension or a manner per the circumstance surrounding a person or situation).

Almost exactly – Their answers are almost the same.

- almost = nearly; exactly = completely or precisely

Deliberate mistake - It was a deliberate mistake so that the deadline would be extended.

- Deliberate means "well-planned"; "mistake" is accidental.

Only choice - That's the only choice given to us.

- Only = one. When there's a choice, there are alternatives or possibilities.

Pretty ugly - The aftermath of the earthquake is pretty ugly.

- Pretty = nice, good-looking; ugly = unpleasant, unattractive.

Random order - He maintains that the selection process was done in a random order.

- Order = organised; random = lacks organisation.

True lies - James Cameron's movie 'True Lies' is about an American spy juggling his work and home life.

- True = is not a lie; lie = is not true.

An oxymoron walked into a bar. The *silence* was *deafening*.

https://upjoke.com/oxymoron-jokes accessed on

Oxymoron or not, <u>avoid double negatives</u>.

A negative form in English is done by adding a negation to the verb. For example, "I can cook tonight" becomes "I cannot cook tonight". In standard English, each subject-predicate phrase should only have one negative form. When negative forms of nouns "nowhere," "nothing," and "no one" are in a sentence, the verb is not negated(e.g. It does nothing).You can't say, "She doesn't know no one. (Correct – "She knows no one" or "She doesn't know someone").

P

(p is pronounced "piː" in UK and US English)

Punctuation!

(It sounds "puhngk·choo·ay·shn")

Let's eat, Chimp. Let's eat Chimp.

P as in the word plate (/pleɪt/)

A plate can be a thin, flat metal sheet or other material for storing a battery or capacitor. Plate tectonics is a section of the Earth's lithosphere in constant motion. Here, a plate is a flat dishware where you eat from or serve food.

("Anniversary" is "birthday" in French. So, he's thinking of either the birthday of one of his parents or the wedding anniversary of his father and mother - parents' anniversary).

The expression "Too much on one's plate" means having a lot to cope with or many things to do, as in the deadline for homework, sitting for the final exam, or preparing a surprise wedding anniversary party for your parents. An overloaded dinner plate is compared to when you're snowed under with activities (i.e. overwhelmed with tasks).

Other versions:

A lot on my plate

Enough on my plate

So much on my plate

Example:

It is hectic for us as we have a lot on our plate.

She has too much on her plate, so don't bother her with organising a family reunion.

A different plate!

More ps

(Not peas)

During our reading comprehension exercise, one **participant** insisted that the verb "pat" is a sleeping synonym for "stab" in his work vocabulary. She said, "Pat on the back" often changes to "stab on the back".

Greg added, "Kick in the **pants**".

Maria: That's not the expression. It's "kick in the …", which is offensive.

Pat on the back is an expression used to show **praise** or approval. Example: Gayle has received a pat from her manager on a successful **presentation** about their department.

To stab in the back is to betray someone or to be disloyal. Her colleague told their supervisor she was again late at the interdepartmental committee meeting. She didn't expect the former to stab her in the back. (Back-stabbing is a noun that means performing betrayal, disloyalty, or treachery).

Ps of Janus

An auto-antonym or contronym is a word that has two contradicting meanings, which is described as "Janus". Janus was an ancient Roman god with two faces looking in opposite directions. In Latin, Janus means doorway or arcade.

Peer is another Janus word that shakes non-native English speakers' brains. It can mean a member of an aristocratic family (e.g. baron, duke, or earl) or a non-royal family member who is a colleague or classmate (i.e. of the same age, social position, or abilities as others in a group).

Peer pressure refers to the influence people of the same social or occupational group have on each other. It is usually used to describe undesirable behaviours, such as drinking alcohol and spending money you don't have. However, it can have positive effects like exercising or studying.

Cambridge University graduation in 2015.

Peer pressure and social norms are powerful influences in education and career.

A TV reporter is interviewing a 103-year-old woman about the secrets of her long life.

He asks, *"What do you think is the best thing about being 103?"*

She replies, *"No peer pressure."*

Q

("q" is pronounced "kju:" in UK and US English)

Question

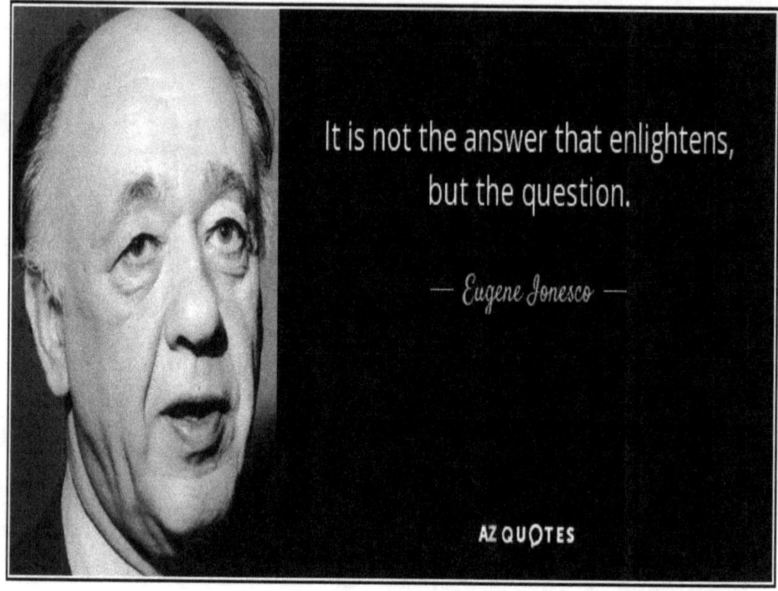

-   https://www.azquotes.com/quotes/topics/asking-questions.html accessed on 23/12/2023

A. To make questions, we often put the verb before the subject, which is called inversion.

Affirmative: They are learning English.

Question: Are they learning English?

B. If we use a question word (why, what, where, how, etc.), we put it before the verb.

Why is her face black? What's on her face?

C. We use the auxiliary verb "did" in the past simple.

Affirmative - She went to Austria.

Question - Did she go to Australia?

D. We use "do" (plural) and "does" (singular) in the present simple.

Do they protest every year?

Does a protest cause chaos?

E. Question tags

(Unlike the British, the Americans prefer "Tag questions" to "Question tags")

Question tags are primarily used in spoken English to confirm positive or negative statements or get a reply from the person you are talking to.

They are contracted short questions at the end of statements: aren't I (and **not** 'am not I)? isn't she?, won't he?, didn't we?, can't she?, are they?, does he?, should he?, will they?, etc.

a) A negative question tag follows a positive statement.

> They can speak English, can't they?

b) A positive question tag follows a negative statement.

> We aren't criticising it, are we?

c) Only pronouns appear in question tags. Hence, if the subject of a sentence is a noun, it should be replaced with a pronoun.

> **Grace** has finished cooking, hasn't **she**?

d) The question tag is positive if a sentence contains a word with a negative meaning (such as hardly, rarely, barely, seldom, never).

> They **rarely** go to the cinema, **do they**?

A truly big question:

<u>What is reality</u>? By Roger Penrose

Can we be sure that the world we experience is not just a figment of our imaginations?

- New Scientist, 2006 (https://www.newscientist.com/article/mg19225780-068-the-biggest-questions-ever-asked/ accessed on 10/02/24)

(UK and US "ɑːr")

Reflexive Pronouns

These are words that end in *-self* (singular) or *-selves* (plural) used when the subject and the object of a sentence are the same (e.g. *I did it myself*). They can act as direct or indirect objects: **myself, yourself, himself, herself, oneself, itself, ourselves, yourselves, and themselves.**

Would you like to get yourself a cup of tea?

(cuppa - slang for cup of tea)

It looks at itself in the mirror and thought, "Wow, I'm a good-looking creature".

We use reflexive pronouns as the object of
a preposition when the object is the same as the subject of
the verb.

We *felt sorry **for** ourselves.*

The children had to look **after** themselves.

We use reflexives with the preposition by (i.e. to show that
someone or they did something without help from others).

Their primary school children went to school **by** themselves.

However, we **don't use reflexives after the preposition of
place.**

The children placed the trolley close to them. It's incorrect
to say, "The children placed the trolley close to themselves".

She will put the book beside her (<u>not</u> "beside herself").

"Beside herself" has a different connotation; it means being
in an extreme and negative emotional state. For instance,
"When her mother died, she was beside herself with grief"
(that is, her mother's death has caused her crisis, and she
was out of control of her normal feelings or emotions).

We use reflexives to emphasise the person, place, or object
being referred to.

**History repeats itself, the
first as tragedy, then as
farce.
Karl Marx (1818-1883),
German-born sociologist**

We often place the reflexive pronoun at the end of the sentence when we are emphasising intensively.

He filled in their income tax return himself.

We use reflexives to show that someone is alone.

She has been living by herself for ages.

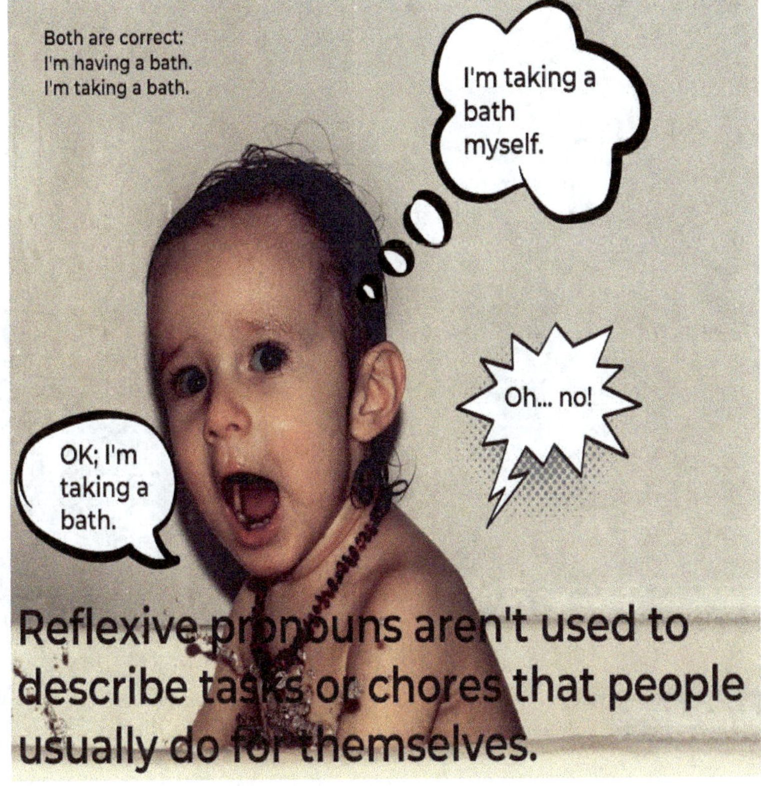

Believe in yourself.

Be yourself.

Take care of yourself.

Laugh at yourself.

S

A synonym (ˈsɪn.ə.nɪm) is a word or phrase that means exactly or nearly the same as another word or phrase.

Can the <u>verb</u> "to approximate" (noun – approximation) and "to estimate" (noun – estimation) be used **synonymously** or interchangeably?

To approximate is to come close (i.e. not completely accurate or equal) to something in nature, quantity, or quality (not for physical distance). If you don't know how many novels you'll sell, it can be approximated by the number of previous books sold last year.

To estimate is to calculate and form an opinion (i.e. a process) regarding the amount, size, weight, worth, etc., of something as close to the actual value as possible. We have estimated the cost of renovating a castle in southern France at 1.5 million euros.

An estimation is an educated guess. "I estimated that they would be home in five hours, but you cannot say, "I approximated that they would be home in five hours".

New Words in 2023	Their Synonyms
Cringe	*awkwardness*

- an uncomfortable situation that causes embarrassment or disgust.

(Cringy – adjective)

Deplatform   *cancelling* (related to
                                        "cancel culture")

-   Removing individuals or groups from a social media
    platform, notably by IT companies, to police hate
    speech and misinformation.

Gaslighting   *manipulating*

-   Tricking people into doubting their own reality

Greenwashing   *false advertising,
                                        environmental
                                        deception*

-   Promoting something environmentally-friendly

    (or less environmentally damaging) than is true to
    gain more customers or improve public image.

Hard pass   *No*

-   A solid yet polite way of saying "no"

Jabbed   *vaxxed*

-   Vaccinated against Covid-19

Permacrisis   *persistent turmoil,
                                        unending disaster*

-   A state of constant crisis

Shrinkflation   *price cheating*

-   A reduction in size of goods, particularly food items,
    whose prices remain the same

Sportswashing   *(I didn't find a word or
                                        two to describe the
                                        practice of
                                        governments,*

companies, groups, or individuals of using sports to improve their reputation tarnished by their wrong policies and actions).

- Using sports to improve a company's or country's image

Sentient

alive (opposite: insentient
– can't feel physical or emotional pain or pleasure).

- Conscious, able to sense

Side hustle

side job, supplementary job

- A secondary source of income

Trip stacking

multiple reservations

- Booking several holidays in the same period

Synonyms aren't metonyms.

Metonyms are words and phrases used as substitutes for closely associated ones (i.e. not the same).

Car is synonymous with "vehicle".

Ride is a metonym for a car.

Example: *Your ride is parked in front of the hotel.*

Common Metonyms

Dish - is a metonym/substitute for a plate of food. *This is my favourite dish.*

Hollywood - is a metonym for the movie industry. *She wants to be in Hollywood.*

Pen - is a metonym for a written text or communications, as in the saying --*The pen is mightier than the sword".*

Sweat - is a metonym for hard work. *It takes a lot of sweat to be a school principal.*

Tongue - is a metonym for language. *What's your mother tongue?*

Turf - is a metonym for an area of expertise. *Have confidence in me; it's my turf.*

Hand - is a substitute for assistance.

Please give him a hand with that; it's too heavy to be lifted by one person.

Anaphora is the antonym (opposite) of epistrophe.

Anaphora is a repetition of a word or more at the beginning of phrases, sentences, or verses for emphasis.

Epistrophe is a repetition of words at the end of
successive phrases, clauses or sentences.

Former US President Barack Obama's speech in 2008
included this phrase: Yes, we *can*. Yes, we *can*. Yes, we *can*.

Who said "…government of *the people*, by *the people*, for
the people"?

- It was Abraham Lincoln, an American lawyer and the
  16th US president from 1861 until his assassination in
  1865.

These are some of the words added to the Merriam-Webster Dictionary in 2023

(https://www.merriam-webster.com/wordplay/new-words-
in-the-dictionary):

Slang and Informal

Doggo (noun) - Dog

Padawan (noun) - A young person, especially when
regarded as naive or inexperienced.

Goated (adjective) - Considered to be the greatest of all time.

TTYL (abbreviation) - Talk to you later.

The Digital World

Generative AI (noun) - Artificial intelligence capable of
generating new content.

Vector graphics (noun) - a process of creating digital images using mathematical formulas to specify the relationship between the elements of the image (such as the start and end points of a line) rather than by defining each pixel.

Smishing (noun) - The practice of sending text messages to someone to trick the person into revealing personal or confidential information, which can then be used for criminal purposes.

The Analog World

UAP (abbreviation) - Unidentified Aerial Phenomenon (a mysterious flying object in the sky that is sometimes assumed to be a spaceship from another planet); also - unidentified anomalous phenomenon (a mysterious phenomenon, mainly an unidentified aerial phenomenon that is sometimes believed to be a spaceship from another planet).

Crate-dig (verb) - To shop for rare, vintage, or obscure recordings, especially by searching through crates of second-hand merchandise.

Jorts (plural noun) - Shorts made of denim or jeans; jean shorts.

Gaming and Other Screens

Cutscene (noun) - A non-interactive video sequence that occurs between segments of a video game and depicts part of the game's background or storyline.

Non-player character (noun) NPC - A character in a video game that does not represent and cannot be manipulated by a player b: a character in a role-playing board game, card game, or live-action game that is controlled or performed by an organiser, facilitator, or supporting participant.

Cold open (noun) - A film or television episode scene that precedes the title sequence or opening credits.

Logline (noun) - A simple synopsis of a screenplay, film, or book used for pitching.

Vanity card (noun) - The logo of a production company that appears briefly on-screen following the credits of a television show or movie.

Culture and Society

Thirst trap (noun) - A photograph (such as a selfie) or video shared to attract attention or desire; also - someone or something that attracts attention or a strong desire.

Grammable (adjective) - Suitable to be posted on the Instagram photo-sharing service.

Doomscroll (verb) - To spend excessive time online scrolling through news or other content that makes one feel sad, anxious, angry, etc.

Quiet quit (verb) - To do the minimum amount of work required for a job; to engage in quiet quitting.

Prosocial (adjective) - Intended to help or benefit another person or group.

To cape (verb) - To act as a defender or supporter.

Chef's kiss (noun) - A gesture of satisfaction or approval made by kissing the fingertips of one hand and then spreading the fingers with an outward motion, often used interjectionally.

Food and the Cooks

Smashburger (noun) - A hamburger patty pressed thin onto a heated pan or griddle at the start of cooking; a patty (as of beans or ground turkey) prepared similarly; or a sandwich featuring one or more such patties.

Stagiaires (noun) - Unpaid interns working in a professional kitchen as part of their training to become chefs (i.e. cooks in restaurants and hotels).

Climate and the Environment

Carbon capture and storage (noun) - Any methods of removing and storing carbon dioxide produced by industrial processes to keep it from entering the atmosphere.

Forever chemical (noun) - A toxic substance, especially a synthetic chemical that persists and accumulates in the environment.

Green chemistry (noun) - An approach to designing and creating chemical processes and products that are safer for humans and the environment and are energy efficient.

Sports and Exercise

Kiss-and-cry (noun) - An area adjacent to a skating rink where figure skaters wait for their marks immediately after performing in a competition.

Tabata (noun) - High-intensity interval training usually consists of eight exercises (such as jumping jacks), each performed at maximum intensity for 20 seconds interspersed with a brief rest of 10 seconds.

Battle rope (noun) - A piece of fitness equipment consisting of a thick, heavy, long rope typically anchored to a solid surface (such as a wall or post) at one end and gripped in hand at the other. This is usually used in pairs in exercises involving moving the arms up and down to cause the ropes to move in continuous waves or slam against the ground.

Bracketology (noun) - The practice or study of predicting the outcome of elimination in tournaments or competitions, especially in NCAA college basketball.

Beast mode (noun) - An extraordinarily aggressive or energetic style or manner that someone (such as an athlete) adopts temporarily to overpower an opponent in a fight or competition.

Doing Business

Meme stock (noun) - A stock that experiences a sudden surge in popularity and price due to a coordinated effort by small investors (such as a viral social media campaign).

Last mile (noun) - The final stage of the distance that must be covered by a service to reach a consumer (such as a telecommunications network or delivery service).

Girlboss (noun) - An ambitious and successful woman (especially a businesswoman or entrepreneur).

Street date (noun) - The date a manufacturer or publisher sets as the first day a product may be sold to consumers.

Microtransaction (noun) - An online transaction involving a small amount of currency, especially a transaction made within a video game (to purchase exclusive content or competitive advantage).

Not-so-new yet uncommonly used:

• Bingo card (noun, slang) - a list of possible, expected, or likely scenarios. *A summer holiday in Australia is on my bingo card.*

- Mid (adjective) - neither good nor bad, so-so. *How was the concert? Mid.*

("Mid" is a commonly used adjective to mean middle or halfway between two points. *It happened at the mid-point of our trip*).

- Quixotic (adjective) - unrealistic or impractical. *They meant well, but their strategies are pretty quixotic given the reduction in their 2024 budget.*

Vigilance in our digitalised world

"Credential stuffing" is stealing login details from one site and trying them on another to see if they work. It is a type of cyberattack where hackers use stolen usernames and passwords to gain unauthorised access to online accounts.

My word of the day:

Absolve (verb) - to free someone from responsibility, commitment, or the consequences of guilt. "The plaintiff asserts that the company is not absolved of responsibility for the false claims simply because its ownership has changed". (Mirriam-Websters, https://www.merriam-webster.com / word-of-the-day accessed on 07/012/20254).

Word of the Year

"Every year, candidates for Word of the Year are debated and one is eventually chosen that is judged to reflect the ethos, mood, or preoccupations of that particular year and to have lasting potential as a word of cultural significance". –

Oxford Languages (https://languages.oup.com/word-of-the-year-faqs/#:~:text=Every%20year%2C%20candidates %20for%20Word,a%20word%20of%20cultural%20signifi cance).

According to Oxford Languages, they draw the candidates for the Word of the Year from data collected monthly through their extensive language research program, including the Oxford Corpus, of around 150 million current English words from web-based publications. They take into account suggestions sent to them via social media, and their Oxford Languages team selects the final Word of the Year based on all the information available to them.

The Preply's survey results show that the 2023 top five commonly used slang terms parents of teenagers are most familiar with are (Zajechowski, M. 2023):

Sus - doubt, suspicion, or questionable. *It looks sus.*

Bet - I agree, I'm sure, for sure, definitely, or good news.

Yeet - To throw something, especially with force and "lack of concern for the thing being thrown. *You don't yeet something if you're worried that it might break.* Yeet is also used as an interjection, most often to express excitement or enthusiasm". Merriam-Webster Dictionary

Salty – Bitter or upset over something. *They're salty because the concert started one hour late.*

T

(UK/US - t /tiː/)

The

If "the" is followed by a consonant sound, it's pronounced \thə\ and is unstressed. For example, the bell, the cat, the garden, and the one (the word *one* begins with the "w" sound, which is a consonant).

If "the" is followed by a vowel sound, it is usually pronounced \thē\, as in "the apple"; however, it is the \thə\ hour because the letter "h" is silent.

"The" is a must with superlative adjectives.

"The" is added to a singular noun to emphasise or make a generalisation about particular animals (e.g. the elephant, the koala), body parts (the mouth, the leg), currencies (the Australian dollar, the euro, the yen), inventions (the mobile phone, the electric car), musical instruments (the guitar, the violin), and plants (the guava tree, the avocado tree).

The koala is a cuddly marsupial native to Australia.

I have corns and calluses on the right foot.

The British pound has lost its value.

The electric car is becoming popular in most cities.

My son plays the guitar.

The avocado tree is not difficult to grow.

"The" is used in a statement or question which has an ordering or ranking phrases, such as "the first", "the second", "the third", "the next", "the last", "the previous", "the following", "the penultimate", etc.

He was the last one to leave the room.

The previous training was more interesting.

"The" can be used with certain adjectives when referring to a group of people, such as "the immigrants, "the teenagers', "the rich", "the elderly", etc.

The elderly live longer but poorer.

However, it is not used when generalising about nationalities or ethnic groups that end in "ans", such as "Australians", "Indians", and "Scandinavians".

Australians are down-to-earth.

"The" is used with names of countries that have "States", "Kingdom", "Republic", "Emirates", "Union", and "Coast" (e.g. The United Kingdom, The Republic of Ireland) and those that end in "s" (e.g. The Bahamas, The Maldives and The Philippines).

I have been to the United States of America.
The European Union is getting stronger every year.

However, **do not use** "the" with states, regions, provinces, and cities unless "the" is part of the name or it includes the word "Territory" or "Coast".

They live in Canberra, Australia.
They live in the Northern Territory.

"The" is used in bridges (*The London bridge is always full of people.*), geographical regions (*I have not been to the Middle East.*), global references (*Where is the South Pole?*), hotels (*The Ritz Hotel*), theatres (*the Metz Theatre*), museums (*The Louvre*), and exceptional works of architecture (*the Eiffel Tower*) and art (*the Last Supper*).

Likewise, it is added to archipelagoes, coasts, deserts, lakes, mountains, oceans, rivers, seas, and swamps.

The Candaba Swamp in the Philippines is composed of freshwater ponds and swamps.

"The" is used when discussing a specific noun in the sentence or followed by a prepositional or relative clause. *Can you give me **the** pencil sharpener on the desk?* (We use "the" because we know which pencil sharpener is being specified. "The" also goes before the desk, as the speaker and listener would know which desk is being referred to).

*Can you give me **a** pencil sharpener? **A** solution must be found. There's **an** eraser on her desk.* "A" is when the word starts with a consonant (e.g. a dog), and "an" is when the term begins with a vowel (e.g. an egg). Words that start with a silent "h" (e.g. hour) take article "an" (She left an hour ago).

"A" and "an" are only used when discussing countable nouns. Countable nouns can be used, like the word "per".

Blueberries cost 4.00 euros per kilo in Poland, whereas they cost 16.00 euros a kilo in France.

My students have told me that, unlike "a" and "an, "the" is not easy to use except in questions and superlative statements (e.g. "the best", "the biggest", "the most important", "the least interesting", etc.).

She is the best colleague I have ever had.

Articles ("an/a" or "the") are not used when generalising about uncountable nouns and plural countable nouns.

Winter in Australia is not cold. (Winter - uncountable noun)

Kangaroos are breeding like rabbits in Australia. (Kangaroos - plural countable nouns)

They're on *a* tourist bus. They're on *the* 9 am tourist bus. They're on *an* electric tourist bus.

Teachers

"A very wise old teacher once said: I consider a day's teaching wasted if we do not all have one hearty laugh".

– Gilbert Highet (A 20th-century humanities teacher in the USA)

i. The phrasal verb "give out" has the following meanings:

To last or work no longer. *Food vouchers will be given out by the end of December 2024.*

To issue or distribute. *They gave out free tickets to the concert.*

To break down or fail. *This lift (US)/elevator (UK English) often gets out of order.*

ii. A sentence is a group of words that starts with a capital letter, usually contains a verb, and forms a statement, question, exclamation, or instruction. *Their English teacher **has written** this sentence on the board: "Past, Present, and Future got into the exam room simultaneously. They looked tense".*

"Has written" is present perfect tense – has (singular) or have (plural) + past participle. Its uses are:

- For something that started in the past and continues in the present (I've been teaching for 12 years).
- When we talk about an experience up to the present (I've taught neuro-diverse university students),
- In negative forms that have "never" (They have never failed the final exams).

A "sentence" also means a judgment or verdict (noun). *The judge gave them a long sentence for burglary.* This is an example when used as a verb: *The judge sentenced them to 25 years in prison for burglary.*

Tree and Elephant

"The tree is more than first a seed, then a stem, then a living trunk, and then dead timber. The tree is a slow, enduring force straining to win the sky." Antoine de Saint-Exupéry (Antoine Marie Jean-Baptiste Roger, (1900 – 1944, French writer and pioneering aviator).

They both have large trunks.

A trunk is a thick main stem of a tree. It's also a word for a long, tube-shaped, flexible nose of an elephant.

The expression *"the elephant in the room"* refers to an obvious problem or situation that no one wants to talk about because they are uneasy or uncomfortable about it. It can also mean an issue or topic everyone knows but feels awkward discussing because it will embarrass an individual, group, government, or organisation. For instance, during an urgent staff meeting, daily tasks and projects were reallocated because of a 41-year-old colleague's death, which was believed to be due to harassment at work. No one spoke about his suicide; no one even mentioned his name.

U

(UK and US - u is pronounced /juː/ but /uː/ in blue)

UK and US English

Correct words might be identified as incorrect depending on the spellchecker, software, or website you use.

"As with so many aspects of language, what you use tends to be the result of a battle between what you were taught, and what you like the look of". "British and American English have more in common than people sometimes think. And you can quote me on that".

- David Marsh (2011).

One of the questions my students often ask is: "Which is better: British or American English?" Most of them write in UK English but use many US words when they speak. I responded, "They are both English, but you should use them consistently in written communication. If you know whether your reader is American or British, use the right kind accordingly." Australians tend to use both, especially when speaking; for instance, they talk about soccer (as in the US) and not football (UK) but go on holiday (as in the UK and not vacation as in the US). In writing, however, they and those from other Commonwealth countries (those with historical or cultural ties with the UK) use British English. Hence, the rule is to be consistent throughout your correspondence or document.

British English is used in the United Kingdom (Scotland, England, North Ireland and Wales), the Republic of Ireland, Australia, Canada, New Zealand and other Commonwealth countries. American English is used in the United States of America (and its former colonies, such as The Philippines), Japan, Korea, Taiwan, Russia, and Eastern Europe.

The differences are:

Spelling

UK - ce, ise, ogue, ou, re and yse

defence, criticise, monologue, labour, centre and analyse

US - er, ize, og, o, se and yze

defense, criticize, monolog, labor, center and analyze

Vocabulary

UK	US
autumn	fall

bill	check
chemist	pharmacy/drugstore
chips	French fries
fizzing drinks	soda
lorry	truck
trousers	pants
post a letter	mail a letter
shop	store
sweets	candies
take away	take out

There are also British words, e.g. advert and barrister, unfamiliar to Americans. Likewise, there are US words that are not used in the UK, such as AC (air conditioning) and stool (waste matter after food has been digested/ excrement/feces – US, faeces - UK).

Collective nouns

Collective nouns have more than one item or person. In UK English, these are considered plural; whereas in US English, they take a singular form.

Band - a group of musicians:

UK – My favourite band are playing this weekend.

US – My favorite band is playing this weekend.

Staff - a group of employees:

UK – Our staff are organised.

US – Our staff is organized.

Team - a group of players:

UK – Their national football team are awesome.

US – Their national soccer team is awesome.

Past Tense of Verbs

Verbs which end in "t" in the UK are commonly spelled with "ed" in US English (spelt/spelled respectively). However, American and British English speakers commonly use the past tense and past participle of irregular verbs dreamt/dreamed and spoilt/spoiled.

The past participle form of the verb 'get' is 'gotten and got' in the US, but it's only 'got' in UK English.

Use of present perfect tense and past tense

Speakers of British English use the present perfect tense (have or has + past participle) in sentences where the past action is significant to the present situation or the action is more important than the time of action, as well as when the sentences contain the words 'already,' 'just' and 'yet'.

I have responded to the email from Angie Loft.

She has already read that book. (We should not give it to her as a birthday present).

Give us time to relax. *We have just arrived.*

Speakers of American English are likely to use simple past in these situations.

I responded to the email from Angie Loft.

She already read that book.

We just arrived.

Modal Verbs

Modal verbs, such as should, shall, must and need, help form a grammatical function. A British person is likely to use "shall" as an alternative to "will" (future form), but an American speaker will say "should". The former uses "need/needn't" while the latter employs "does/do".

UK - Shall we close the window? (Shall is used only with the pronouns "I" and "we")

US - Should we close the window? (Americans never use "shall" with the pronouns "I" and "we")

UK - He needn't go to church with me if he doesn't want to.

US - He does not have to go to church with me if he doesn't want to. (They do not need to go to church).

When replying to questions in British English, "do" is used instead of a verb.

Are they going home soon?

They might do.

Whereas the American speakers omit the "do".

They might.

Use and non-use of prepositions

In British English, "at" is used with time expressions and when talking about universities and similar institutions.

I will be there at seven in the morning.

We usually get together at Easter.

They had a party at the weekend.

I studied sociology at university.

In American English, "on" is used when talking about the weekend and "in" with universities and other institutions.

They had a party on the weekend.

I studied sociology in high school and university.

In British English, "to" and "from" are used with the adjective "different".

He is so different from any other men I have met.

He is so different to other men I have met.

The Americans, however, use "from" and "than" with "different".

He is different from any other men I have met.

He is different than other men I have met.

(Also, it is common to hear "different to" because of people confusing it with "similar to").

In British English, "to" is used after the verb "write", which is not the case in American English.

I will write to you as soon I have the timetable. (UK)

I will write you as soon as I have the timetable. (US)

Dates

The UK, Europe and other countries use the day-month-year format without commas.

I left Australia on 5 February 2024. (05/02/24)

The US use the month-day-year format with a comma after the day and year.

I left Australia on February 5, 2024. (02/05/24)

When there's "of", use an ordinal number, which can also be spelt out.

I left England on the 5th of February 2024.

I left the USA on the fifth of February 2024.

Poundland is a British variety store chain that sells inexpensive items priced at one pound.

In America, they have dollar stores.

"England and America are two countries separated by the same language".

- George Bernard Shaw (1856 - 1950, Irish playwright, political activist, and 1925 Nobel Prize in Literature awardee).

V

(UK/US pronunciation of v is /viː/ as in very)

Verbs

Kinds of Verbs
Action verbs
Auxiliary verbs (helping verbs)
Stative verbs
Modal verbs
Transitive verbs
Intransitive verbs
Linking verbs
Regular verbs
Irregular verbs
Phrasal verbs
Infinitives

Action verbs

These refer to physical actions performed with our bodies or objects, such as cooking and writing. They can be regular or irregular verbs (a list of these is provided later).

They're writing on smartphones because writing on paper isn't cool anymore.

Stative verbs

These refer to conditions or situations and describe beliefs, emotions, qualities, states of existence, and opinions (e.g. has/have (past tense – had), love, own, and want).

She had an unexpected guest on Friday, the 13th.

Transitive verbs (can be action or static verbs)

These are accompanied by a direct object, a noun, pronoun or noun phrase that is the receiver of the sentence's subject's action.

*They **watered** the indoor plants in our office. (action verb).*

*We **want** organic ingredients for all dishes served at the cafeteria. (static verb)*

Helping verbs (auxiliary verbs)

These are helpful verbs that work with other verbs to change the meaning of a sentence; they may alter the verb tense or mood of a sentence. The common helping verbs are can, do, will, and verb-to-be.

Yes, we can!

They have not done it.

Intransitive verbs

These are the opposites of transitive verbs (**they do not have direct objects**).

The mice play while the cat is away.

Linking verbs

They link a subject with its complement and function as intransitive verbs (i.e. do not take direct objects): appear, be, become, look, seem, and verb to be.

They appear motivated to do this project.

I am a great dancer.

Modal verbs

They are a subgroup of helping verbs that are used for specific moods, expressing ability (can), necessity (must), possibility (might, would), or permission (may). Modal verbs are explained in detail in another section.

We must not be late for the meeting.

Phrasal verbs

They comprise a verb and one or two participles (preposition, adverb, or both). Their meaning is different from that of their separate parts.

Bring up = start talking about a particular subject (We didn't bring up the issue about pay raise at the last meeting.

Fill in = complete or write information in a form or document (She filled in the questionnaire yesterday).

Come across = to find something by chance (My friend came across your book at the Amnesty International Book Fair.

... The rest is on your hand.

Phrasal verbs have literal and metaphorical/ figurative meanings.

They should have bought into the idea of electric cars. (present tense - phrasal verb "buy into" means believe in).

(UK/US pronunciation of w is /ˈdʌb.əl.juː/)

Wisdom

(UK/US - ˈwɪz.dəm)

If it isn't broken, don't fix it.

"A young man was searching for the secret of wisdom and heard that there was a guru high in the Himalayas who knew. So he set off to find the guru, going through much hardship and travail until finally, high in the mountains, he found the Master sitting in the lotus posture.

"Tell me, oh Master!" he cried. "What is the secret of wisdom?"

The Master replied: "Good judgment."

"But how do you get good judgment?" asked the young man.

The Master replied: "Experience."

"And how do you get experience?" the young man persisted.

"Ah," said the Master: "Bad judgment."

- https://www.sandylillie.com/humor.html 27/01/24

What's up on WhatsApp? (Knowledge and Wisdom are chatting)

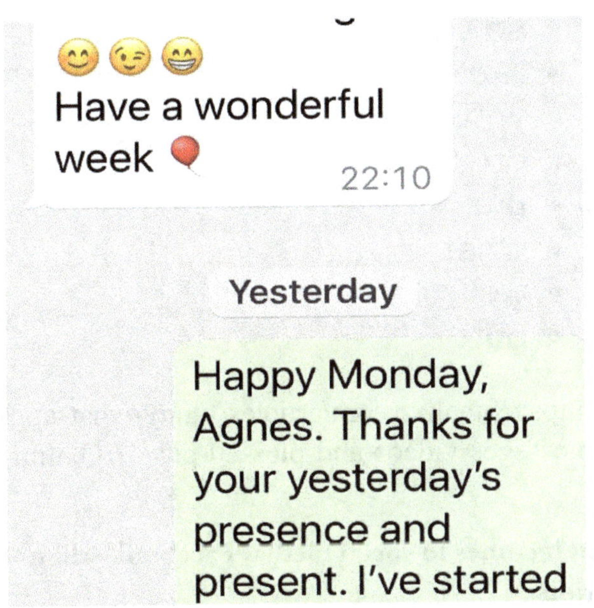

Recently, when asked about managing experience at her job interview, Joanna told the recruiters that she manages their family's Whatsapp group.

Currently, WhatsApp is free; how long for, no one knows! It's my only online presence; I'm not present on other social media platforms.

Below is a WhatsApp message from Funalive:

99.9% of my sentences start with

- oh my god
- yeah
- no
- basically
- wait
- so yeah
- like
- you know
- oh
- um
- what
- well
- but

\-   https://funalive.com/articles/funny-whatsapp-jokes-messages-videos-and-pics-20-pics_7rQ.html)

When it comes to social media, Facebook still holds the top position.

Since Facebook claims ownership of everything you post on their website, I think I should start uploading my bills.

—   https://upjoke.com/facebook-jokes

Regarding dating applications, LinkedIn is the worst because everyone wants to talk only about their work, projects, and views on success.

About Twitter (now X), what shall I call the current tweets? Twix? Xeet? Xes? Xpost? X is easier used as a verb because contributors are encouraged to use active rather than passive voice (e.g. I've Xed about the pneumonoultramicroscopicsilicovolcanokoniosis   – the longest word in the English language, which refers to a lung disease caused by inhaling ash and sand dust).

"What's the difference between Reddit and Instagram? Reddit fills your mind with thoughts. Instagram fills your mind with thots".

- https://upjoke.com/instagram-jokes accessed on 03/01/2024

Thot/s is a slang and offensive word that refers to a promiscuous woman. It's sexist; changing "woman" to "person" doesn't make it acceptable, even in informal conversations. "Thot" also stands for "That Ho Over There"; "Ho" is a short form for "whore" – a prostitute. *Hence, please don't use it; it's only here to make a point.*

"I finally know why tiktok is still popular. - Because one man's trash, is another man's treasure".

- https://upjoke.com/tiktok-jokes accessed 18/01/2024

X

(UK and US pronunciation of x is /eks/, as in X-ray /eks.reɪ/)

X-ray is a photographic or digital image of the internal composition of something, e.g. part of the body.)

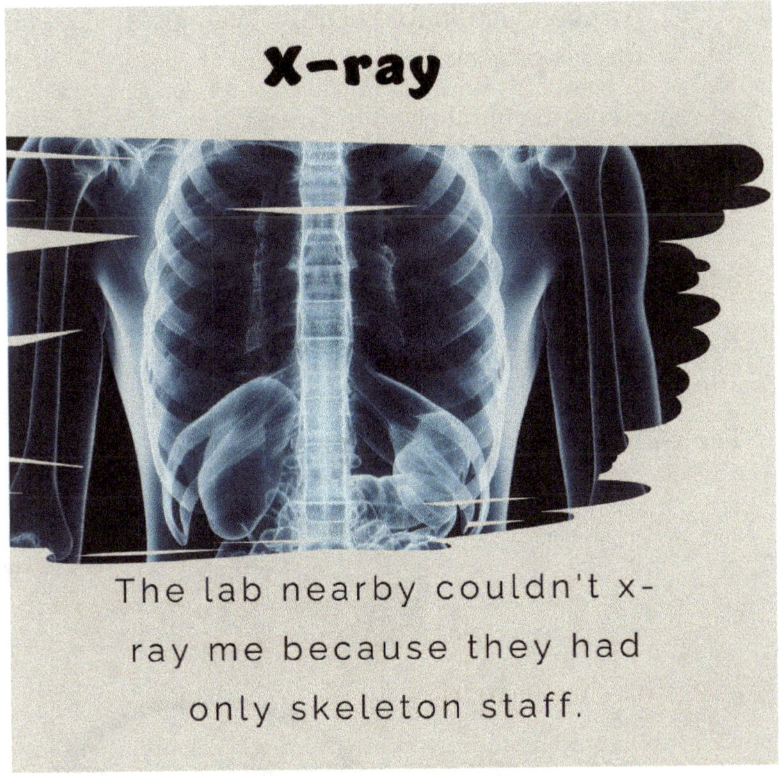

Skeleton staff means there's a minimum number of personnel who operate and maintain a service or organisation.

We use "X" when we cross out or delete something.

Ex, which is pronounced "eks" like the letter X, has several meanings:

- Former = previous: former spouse, former colleague, former job, former address, etc.
- Out of = not anymore: ex-convict, ex-president, etc.
- A shortcut for "example" - They impact international business. Ex. They can disrupt air cargo industry.
- An abbreviation for "extra" - We must find ex cash for this project.

XI represents the number 60 in Greek.

XO (or XOXO) means kisses and hugs. We write this below our names when writing to family and friends.

Some words that start with X are:

Xanthic is an adjective for yellowish. *I think he looks a little **xanthic**.*

The ***x-axis*** is a horizontal line on a graph.

Xenophobia - fear or distrust of people because of their ethnicity or because they seem foreign to you. *She seems xenophobic to me.*

Xerox - to copy a document, which has been made redundant by the advent of new technology. *We used to xerox all documents.*

XHTML is a programming language that expands from the HTML coding language. XML and XSLT are also programming languages. *My friend's husband is an XHTML, XML, and XSLT expert.*

Xylophone is a musical instrument.

XYZ is used when giving an example or talking about something in general.

Y

(UK and US pronunciation of "y" - waɪ)

Yukon in Canada

Yukon is a 482,443-square-kilometre (186,272-square-mile) area in northwest Canada with a population of 40,232 (in 2021); its capital is Whitehorse. About one-fourth of the people there are American Indians (First Nations). - Dr Kenneth John Rea (Professor Emeritus of Economics, University of Toronto ("Yukon Territory", 2023, https://www.britannica.com/place/Yukon-territory accessed 29/12/2023).

English is the most common language spoken in Yukon. Its First Nations, however, are revitalising their Indigenous languages (Gwich'in; Hän; Kaska; Northern Tutchone; Southern Tutchone; Tagish; Upper Tanana; and Tlingit) (https://yukon.ca/en/statistics-and-data/diverse-territory accessed on 29/12/2023).

Although Canadian English is close to American English and has inherited a fair bit from the British, it is uniquely Canadian.

According to Emily Hitz, these are some of the differences between Canadian and American English (https://www.phrasemix.com/answers/how-are-canadian-english-and-american-english-different accessed on 29/12/2023):

"About" or "a boat"

Canadians pronounce words with "ou" differently; for example, when they say out, about, and house, they sound like "oat", "a boat", or "hose".

Eh? and Hey?

Canadians have the habit of saying "eh"; with a rising tone when it is this at the end of a sentence.

It's awesome, eh?

The younger generation sometimes uses "hey" instead of "eh". You're from South Africa, hey?

Sorry

"In Canada, 'sorry rhymes with 'story'. In the USA, it rhymes with 'Ferrari'".

Canadians often say "sorry" much more than Americans, like the British. There's an anecdote that if you step on a Canadian or British foot (i.e., it's your fault), they will say sorry to you.

Pronunciation

"Some words with an 'a' in the middle have a different pronunciation north of the border. For example, let's look at the word 'pasta'. In the USA, the first syllable rhymes with 'lost'. In Canada, it sounds like the past'. We see this difference with the word 'drama' and names like 'Mario, ' 'Natasha,' and 'Alana'. (Most of these are 'borrowed' words that come from other languages.)"

With the word "avenue", Canadians and British people always say "nyew", whereas Americans sometimes pronounce the last part as "new". "Produce" (fruits and vegetables) is sometimes pronounced with the first part rhyming with "saw" in the former while with "go" in the latter. Mom (US) and mum (UK) are used in Canada and pronounced accordingly.

Spelling and Vocabulary

Canadians spell many words in British English, e.g. neighbour (adding "u") and centre ("re" and not "er"). The differences between UK and US English are discussed in another section.

They often say "pardon me" or "pardon", while Americans are more likely to say "excuse me".

They call the toilet "washroom" instead of "loo"/"bathroom" in the UK and "restroom" in the USA.

"Pop" is used in Canada to refer to a sweet, bubbly drink. In the northern USA, particularly in the mid-west, this is a "soft drink", a "soda", or a "coke." (In some places, people say "coke", even for other drinks like 7UP or Fanta).

Canadians say "grade one" or "grade seven", e.g. Canadian high schoolers are from grade nine to grade twelve, whereas the Americans have "first grade" or "ninth grade". The latter call the high school and university years "freshman year", "sophomore year", "junior year", and "senior year". Canadians don't use these terms; for high school, they say "grade nine" to "grade twelve"; for university, they say "first year" to "fourth year";

In Canada, "university" describes an institution with four-year Bachelor courses, especially if it has graduate programmes. In the USA, "college" is a more common term, and "community college" for a school that offers a certificate or non-bachelor programme.

These are Emily's final words:

"It's true that Canadians speak a little bit differently than Americans, sometimes. It's also true that people from Vancouver speak a little differently than people from Toronto. And between the two countries, people from Portland sound a lot like people from Vancouver, and people from Minnesota sound a lot like people from Manitoba. And of course, every individual speaks a bit differently from the next individual. It's very difficult to find many general rules for Canadian and American English differences. *And you don't need to worry — it doesn't matter what kind of English you speak. If Americans understand you, Canadians will too.*"

American, Australian, British, and Canadian native speakers do not understand each other all the time. There are differences in what words and how they say these to convey the same message, as shown in these YouTube videos:

- English differences Among 4 countries! American, British, Aussie, Canadian. Https://www.youtube.com/ watch? v=ajmH5iXWUPU.

- British vs American vs Canadian ENGLISH Differences. Https://www.youtube.com /watch?v = ZI5btv2VFvk.

- 11 English Accents from Around the World in 1 Video. Https://www.youtube.com/watch? v=8dGl_9Kk18c.

I don't *reinvent the wheel* (i.e. I don't waste my time and energy creating something that already exists). Thus, here's an article demonstrating how native English speakers can be alike yet different.

The difference between Aussies, Canadians, Americans and Brits by Starts at 60 Writers

"Aussies: Believe you should look out for your mates.

Brits: Believe that you should look out for those people who belong to your club.

Americans: Believe that people should look out for and take care of themselves.

Canadians: Believe that that is the government's job.

Aussies: Dislike being mistaken for Pommies (Brits) when abroad.

Canadians: Are rather indignant about being mistaken for Americans when abroad.

Americans: Encourage being mistaken for Canadians when abroad.

Brits: Can't possibly be mistaken for anyone else when abroad.

Canadians: Endure bitterly cold winters and are proud of it.

Brits: Endure oppressively wet and dreary winters and are proud of it.

Americans: Don't have to do either, and couldn't care less.

Aussies: Don't understand what inclement weather means.

Americans: Drink weak, pissy-tasting beer.

Canadians: Drink strong, pissy-tasting beer.

Brits: Drink warm, beery-tasting piss.

Aussies: Drink anything with alcohol in it.

Americans: Seem to think that poverty and failure are morally suspect.

Canadians: Seem to believe that wealth and success are morally suspect.

Brits: Seem to believe that wealth, poverty, success, and failure are inherited.

Aussies: Seem to think that none of this matters after several beers.

Brits: Have produced many great comedians, celebrated by Canadians, ignored by Americans, and therefore not rich.

Aussies: Have produced comedians like Paul Hogan and Yahoo Serious.

Canadians: Have produced many great comedians such as John Candy, Martin Short, Jim Carrey, Dan Akroyd, and all the rest at SCTV.

Americans: Think that these people are American!

Americans: Spend most of their lives glued to the idiot box.

Canadians: Don't, but only because they can't get more American channels.

Brits: Pay a tax just so they can watch 4 channels.

Aussies: Export all their crappy programs, which no one there watches, to Britain, where everybody loves them.

Americans: Will jabber on incessantly about football, baseball and basketball.

Brits: Will jabber on incessantly about cricket, soccer and rugby.

Canadians: Will jabber on incessantly about hockey, hockey, hockey, and how they beat the Americans twice, playing baseball.

Aussies: Will jabber on incessantly about how they beat the Poms in every sport they played them in.

Aussies: Are extremely patriotic about their beer.

Americans: Are flag-waving, anthem-singing, and obsessively patriotic to the point of blindness.

Canadians: Can't agree on the words to their anthem, in either language, when they can be bothered to sing them.

Brits: Do not sing at all but prefer a large brass band to perform the anthem.

Brits: Are justifiably proud of the accomplishments of their past citizens.

Americans: Are justifiably proud of the accomplishments of their present citizens.

Canadians: Prattle on about how some of those great Americans were once Canadian.

Aussies: Waffle on about how some of their past citizens were once Outlaw Pommies, but none of that matters after several beers".

(https://startsat60.com/ media /lifestyle/jokes/the-difference -between-aussies-canadians-americans-and-brits accessed on 06/01/2024).

How about the Kiwis?

The people of New Zealand

English is the most common spoken language in Aotearoa New Zealand. Māori and New Zealand Sign Language have special status under the law as official languages. Aside from English and te reo Māori, Northern Chinese (including Mandarin) and Hindi are widely spoken (New Zealand Ministry for Ethnic Communities, 2024).

A country in Oceania with a population of over five million, New Zealand is revered for its progressive society, easy-going lifestyle (like in the Oz), and beautiful landscape. My first work manager in Australia was from Wellington, the capital of New Zealand, and he used to say, "I'm not as nutty as you Aussies, but I can laugh with both sense and nonsense".

New Zealand English is similar to Australian English. However, there are slight differences with pronunciation, as in fish and chips sounding like "fush and chups" to the Australians. Unlike the Aussies, the Kiwis always reply to a question or emphasise a point by a rising intonation at the end of the phrase or sentence. The latter also often use words and phrases from Māori, such as haka (dance), kia ora (a greeting), and puku (stomach).

The Kiwis and the Aussies have common slang, for example:

- Ay "eh" - is a particle added to the end of a sentence. It can also mean anything from "Could you repeat that?" to "What do you think?". *"It's hot today, ay"* (i.e. "right" or "you know").
- Bro - in place of mate, man, or dude. *"No worries, bro!"*
- Dunny - another word for toilet. *"Where's the dunny?"*
- Togs - swimmers or swimsuits. *"Bring the children's togs and jandals (flip flops)"*.
- Yeah, nah – The Aussies and Kiwis are exceptionally agreeable; thus, even when they disagree with you, they'll throw in a "yeah", which is a non-committal "no". *"Come to our place for a Barbie"*. "Yeah, nah, we'll think about it ay."

Kiwi slang:

Kia Ora - *Hello* in Maori.

Bach - a holiday house, usually small and simple, close to the beach. *Your girlfriend has a bach, doesn't she?*

Chilly bin – a portable cooler used for chilling stuff ("stuff – an object, food, or anything that you don't have a word for or are too lazy to think about it). We, Australians, call this an "esky". *Don't forget to bring the chilly bin.*

Dairy - a convenience or corner store. *I'm getting milk at the dairy.*

Hard case – a funny person or someone known for outrageous behaviour. *Luca's a hard case; such a joker.*

Snags – sausages. *No worries, I'll throw some snags on the barbie.*

Squiz - to have a quick look at something. *Take/Have a squiz at this, bro!*

Tu meke - too much. It's used to express gratitude for generous acts or words. "Let me get you a cuppa (cup of tea)" *Ah tu meke, mate!*

Yarn - chat, conversation. *I am just dropping by* to *have a yarn.*

Kiwi: Just woke up, mate, or dropping by for a last drink before bed?
Aussie: I'll still be here after you've gone, mate.
Kiwi: How did you lose a slipper?
Aussie: Nah, yeah, I found one!
(In Queensland, the locals say "nup" for no).

Z

For you to be reading this book, you're a **zealous** user of the English language. You'll soon be a **Z**en master of your English communication.

(Antonio Banderas' real name is José Antonio Domínguez Bandera. He's a Spanish actor and director; his quote above was taken from https://www.ef.com/wwen/english-resources/english-quotes/language/ accessed on 25/01/2024).

"My accent was horrible.
In Mexico, nobody says, 'You speak English with a good
accent'.
You either speak English or you don't: As long as you
can communicate, no one cares".
- Salma Hayek (September 2003 issue of O, The Oprah Magazine in https://www.oprah.com/omagazine/oprah-interviews-actress-and-producer-salma-hayek_1/2 seen on 26/12/2023).

"Learning is not a spectator sport.
– D. Blocher

If you want to master English, get involved and practise as much as possible".

(https://englishlive.ef.com/en/blog/english-in-the-real-world/19-motivational-quotes-keep-learning-english/ accessed on 26/12/2023).

There's always something to learn and smile at!

"Erection" (noun) UK/US /ɪˈrek.ʃən/ – The act of building or making a structure. They approved the erection of an electric fence around the prison.

When a man has an erection, his penis is temporarily harder and bigger than usual and points up. https://dictionary.cambridge.org/dictionary/english/erection accessed on 07/01/2024.

Giveaway:

James Harbeck's article "How the English language became such a mess" is fascinating (https://www.bbc. Com /culture/article/20150605-your-language-is-sinful, 8th June 2015).

This is one of his thought-provoking paragraphs: "The problem begins with the alphabet itself. Building a spelling system for English using letters that come from Latin – despite the two languages not sharing exactly the same set of sounds – is like building a playroom using an IKEA office set. But from Tlingit to Czech, many other languages that sound nothing like Latin do well enough with versions of the Latin alphabet".

His text exposes how the English language is a mishmash of parlances and vernaculars. For instance, he says, "Once the English tossed out the French (but not their words) a few centuries later, they started to acquire territories around the world – America, Australia, Africa, India. With each new colony, Britain acquired words: hickory, budgerigar, zebra, bungalow. The British also did business with everyone else and took words as they went – something we call "borrowing," even though the words were kept. Our language is a museum of conquests".

References

Abdelnour, Z K (n.d.). AZQuotes.com, Wind and Fly LTD, 2024. Https://www.azquotes.com/quote/810768, accessed January 04/01/2024.

Berthier, R (2022). English Language Lovers: Teaching, learning, and conversing before and during the pandemic. The EU: France (Printed in Poland).

Broster, H (2019). False Friends in English and Italian. Https://dailyitalianwords.com/a-list-of-20-false-friends-in-english-and-italian/ accessed on 05/01/2024.

Cambridge Dictionary (n.d.). Https://dictionary.cambridge.org/dictionary/english/erection accessed on 07/01/2024.

Coughland, E (2023). Lost in translation! Tourists share hilarious signs they've spotted around the world that have been converted into English (with some VERY odd results). Https://www.dailymail.co.uk/femail/article-11640975/Tourists-share-hilarious-translated-signs-theyve-spotted-world.html accessed on 22/01/2024.

Donald, L (n.d.).
Https://www.brainyquote.com/topics/ranking-quotes accessed on 05/01/2024.

Dyvik, E (2023). The most spoken languages worldwide in 2023. Https://www.statista.com/statistics/266808/the-most-spoken-languages-worldwide/ accessed on 06/02/2024.

Education First (n.d.). Quotes about the English Language. Https://www.ef.com/wwen/english-resources/english-quotes/language/ accessed on 25/01/2024.

Financial Review (2023). Austria or Australia? The truth behind the viral internet meme. Https://www.afr.com/companies/media-and-marketing/austria-or-australia-the-truth-behind-the-viral-internet-meme-20231107-p5ei9z accessed on 06/02/2024.

Government of Yukon (n.d.).
Https://yukon.ca/en/statistics-and-data/diverse-territory accessed on 29/12/2023.

Hanks, P (Ed) (1985). Collins English Dictionary. Sydney, Auckland, Glasgow: William Colllins Sons & Co. Ltd.

Harbeck, J (2015). How the English language became such a mess. Https://www.bbc.com/culture/article/20150605-your-language-is-sinful accessed on 21/12/2023.

Hayek, S (2003).The Oprah Magazine. Https://www.oprah.com/omagazine/oprah-interviews-actress-and-producer-salma-hayek_1/2 seen on 26/12/2023.

Hitz, E (n.d.). How are Canadian English and American English different? Https://www.phrasemix.com/answers/how-are-canadian-english-and-american-english-different accessed on 29/12/2023.

Jones, E (n.d.). "Where does the phrase 'going Dutch' originate?" Https://www.theguardian.com/notesandqueries/query/0,5753-68084,00.html accessed on 31/12/2023.

Kolkman, M (2020). English words you didn't know came from Dutch. Https://www.iamexpat.nl/education/education-news/english-words-you-didnt-know-came-dutch#:~:text=Anchovy accessed on 31/12/2023.

Mahwan (2021). Https://www.reddit.com/r/AskEurope/comments/k8xdfd/false_friends_of_a_translator_what_are_the/?rdt=50239 accessed on 18/01/2024.

Marsh, D (2011). 'The British style'? 'The American way?' They are not so different. Https://www.theguardian.com/media/mind-your-language/2011/may/19/mind-your-language-punctuation-quotations accessed on 25/01/2024.

Mirriam-Websters Dictionary. Https://www.merriam-webster.com/word-of-the-day accessed on 07/012/20254.

Merriam-Webster Dictionary. Https://www.merriam-webster.com/dictionary/yeet accessed on 05/02/2024.

New Scientist (2006. Https://www.newscientist.com/article/mg19225780-068-the-biggest-questions-ever-asked/ accessed on 10/02/24.

New Zealand Ministry for Ethnic Communities (2024). Our Languages - Ō Tātou Reo. Https://www.ethniccommunities.govt.nz/resources/our-languages-o-tatou-reo/ accessed on 06/02/2024.

Rea, K J (2023). Yukon Territory. Https://www.britannica.com/place/Yukon-territory accessed 29/12/2023.

United Nations' Department of Economic and Social Affairs (2023). UN DESA Policy Brief No. 153: India overtakes China as the world's most populous country.

Https://www.un.org/development/desa/dpad/publication/un-desa-policy-brief-no-153-india-overtakes-china-as-the-worlds-most-populous-country/ accessed on 30/12/2023.

Vladraptor, 2021. Https://www.reddit.com/r/Ask Europe /comments /k8xdfd/ false_friends _of _ a_translator _what_are_the/ accessed on 18/01/2024.

Zajechowski, M. 2023. Text slang of 2023: Surveying parents of teens on the latest slang Https://preply.com/en/blog/text-slang-of-2023/ accessed 04/02/2024.

Aphorisms, metaphors, meanings, quotes, and challenging words:

Https://www.azquotes.com/quotes/topics/genuineness.html accessed on 09/02/2024.

Https://www.azquotes.com/quotes/topics/asking-questions.html accessed on 23/12/2023.

Cambridge Dictionary Online (n.d.). Https://dictionary.cambridge.org/pronunciation/accessed December 2023 - January 2024.

Https://www.dictionary.com/e/slang/going-dutch/ accessed on 31/12/2023.

Https://englishlive.ef.com/en/blog/english-in-the-real-world/19-motivational-quotes-keep-learning-english/ accessed on 26/12/2023.

Https://www.goodreads.com/quotes/957891-never-make-fun-of-someone-who-speaks-broken-english-it (H. Jackson Brown Jr.) accessed on 01/01/2024.

Https://www.thelifevirtue.com/metaphors-about-life/ accessed on 25/12/2023.

Https://examples.yourdictionary.com/examples-of-euphemism.html?msclkid accessed on 01/01/2024.

Merriam-Webster Dictionary. Https://www.merriam-webster.com/wordplay/new-words-in-the-dictionary accessed on 18/01/2024.

Merriam-Webster Dictionary. Https://www.merriam-webster.com/dictionary/folk#:~:text=Synonyms%20of%20folk-,1,class%2C%20or%20group%20of%20people.

Jokes and anecdotes:

Didion, J. Https://www.brainyquote.com/topics/grammar-quotesaccessed on 03/01/2024.

Funalive (2022). Funny WhatsApp Jokes, Messages, Videos and Pics - 20 Pics. Https://funalive.com/articles/funny-whatsapp-jokes-messages-videos-and-pics-20-pics_7rQ.html accessed on 02/01/2024.

Gitomer, J (n.d.). Https://www.brainyquote.com/topics/grammar-quotes accessed on 03/01/2024.

Https://www.englishclub.com/esl-jokes/3-heavenandhell-q.php accessed on 28/12/2023.

Https://upjoke.com/facebook-jokes accessed on 03/01/2024.

Https://upjoke.com/genuine-jokes accessed on 28/12/2023.

Https://upjoke.com/instagram-jokes accessed on 03/01/2024.

Https://upjoke.com/oxymoron-jokes accessed on 25/12/2023.

Https://upjoke.com/peer-jokes accessed 09/01/2024.

Https://upjoke.com/possess-jokes accessed on 04/01/2024.

Https://upjoke.com/tiktok-jokes accessed 18/01/2024.

Lillie, S (n.d.). Https://www.sandylillie.com/humor.html accessed on 27/01/2024.

Reader's Digest (n.d.). Https://www.rd.com/list/grammar-jokes/ and //www.rd.com/jokes/money/ accessed on 10/02/2024.

Thunderclogs, CountPenguin, and Rmvandink (2019). Https://www.reddit.com/r/learndutch/comments/gxwf0j/a_nederengels_joke/?rdt=53532 accessed 31/12/2023.

Wittgenste, L (n.d.).
Https://www.brainyquote.com/topics/grammar-quotesaccessed on 03/01/2024.

YADAV, P (2018). 25 Indians Who Should Be Jailed For The Murder Of English Language.
Https://www.scrolldroll.com/indians-who-murdered-english/ accessed on 03/01/2024.

Saying goodbye (farewell)

See you later.

See you soon.

Bye (Bye bye - sweet and childish expression)

I've got to be going

I must be going.

Take it easy.

Have a nice day.

PS:

(PS is an abbreviation for "postscript", which was derived from the Latin word "postscriptum," meaning "write after", and is used to add extra information at the end of your message).

Keep smiling and learn your irregular verbs regularly.

Irregular Verbs

Infinitive	Past Simple	Past Participle
be	was/were	been/gone
beat	beat	beaten
become	became	become

begin	began	begun
bend	bent	bent
break	broke	broken
bring	brought	brought
build	built	built
burn	burned	burned/burnt
buy	bought	bought
can/able	could	could/been
catch	caught	caught
choose	chose	chosen
come	came	come
cost	cost	cost
cut	cut	cut
do	did	done
draw	drew	drawn
dream	dreamed/dreamt	dreamed/dreamt
drink	drank	drunk

drive	drove	driven
eat	ate	eaten
fall	fell	fallen
feel	felt	felt
fight	fought	fought
find	found	found
fly	flew	flown
forget	forgot	forgotten
get	got	got/gotten
give	gave	given
go	went	gone/been
grow	grew	grown
hang	hung/hanged	hung/hanged
have	had	had
hear	heard	heard
hide	hid	hidden

hit	hit	hit
hold	held	held
hurt	hurt	hurt
keep	kept	kept
know	knew	known
learn	learned/learnt	learned/learn
leave	left	left
lend	lent	lent
light	lit	lit
lose	lost	lost
make	made	made
mean	meant	meant
meet	met	met
must	had to	had to
oversleep	overslept	overslept
pay	paid	paid
put	put	put

ride	rode	ridden
read	read (rɛd)	read (rɛd)
ride	rode	ridden
ring	rang	rung
run	ran	run
say	said	said
see	saw	seen
sell	sold	sold
send	sent	sent
set off	set off	set off
shake	shook	shaken
shine	shone	shone
show	showed	shown
shut	shut	shut
sing	sang	sung
sink	sank	sunk

sit	sat	sat
sleep	slept	slept
smell	smelled/smelt	smelled/smelt
speak	spoke	spoken
spend	spent	spent
spread	spread	spread
stand	stood	stood
steal	stole	stolen
sting	stung	stung
swim	swam	swum
take	took	taken
teach	taught	taught
tear	torn	torn
tell	told	told
think	thought	thought
throw	threw	thrown
understand	understood	understood

wake	woke	woken
wear	wore	worn
win	won	won
write	wrote	written

How about regular verbs?

A regular verb, in its past simple and past participle forms, follows this standard pattern: verb + ed.

For example:
instruct – instructed
walk – walked
zip - zipped

They participated in last week's workshop on well-being. (Also correct: wellbeing).

Pronunciation of verbs in the past simple tense --

i) If the last letter of the regular verb ends in a voiced consonant or a vowel sound, pronounce the "ed" as /d/, e.g. believed and cared.

ii) If the last letter of the regular verb ends in a voiceless consonant, pronounce the "ed" as just /t/, e.g. helped and watched.

iii)   If the regular verb ends in either a "t" or a "d"
        sound, pronounce the "ed" as /id/, e.g. decided
        and wanted.

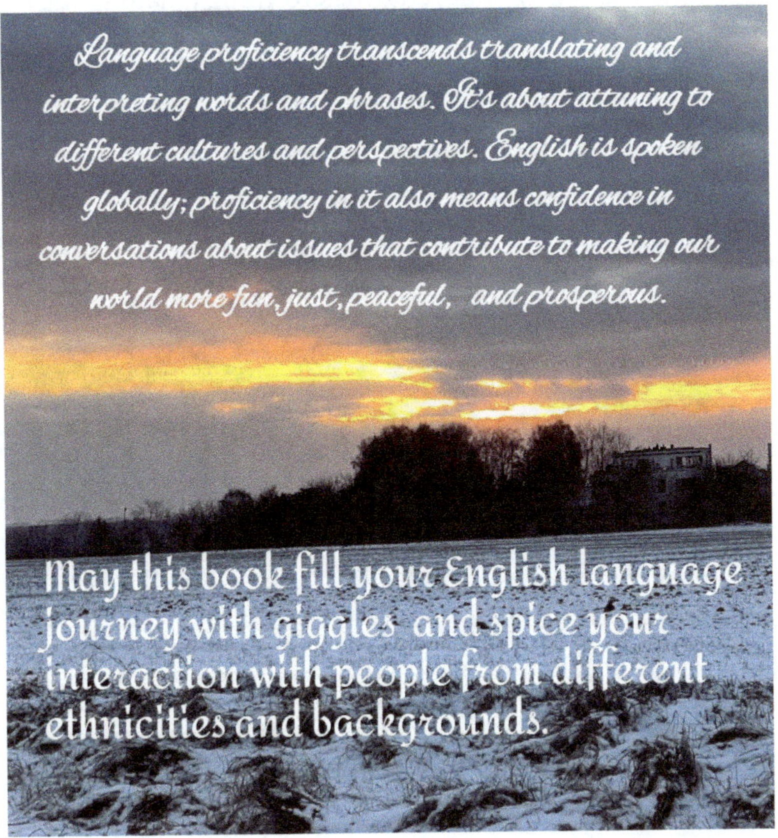

That's all folks!

"Can I use 'folks' in meetings? Isn't it informal?

Merriam-Webster Dictionary (https://www.merriam
webster.com/dictionary/folk#:~:text

=Synonyms) defines "folk" (folks - plural) - noun - as:

• people generally

- a certain kind, class, or group of people

- "persons of one's own family" (sic)

  (*people of the same family*)

- a group of kindred tribes forming a nation

A fox (UK & US pronunciation - /fɒks/) is a small mammalian carnivore that hunts and eats live prey, such as rabbits, squirrels and mice.

Bear in mind: Avoid "folks" in formal written and verbal communication.

As an adjective, folks are ordinary people of a country or region who typically reflect their lifestyle (folk hero, folk music).

Languages change, so although "folks" like "guys" (plural) are informal words, you hear these two words more and more in professional conversations. "Folks" is a friendly alternative to "these people", which sounds blunt and sometimes rude (e.g. Hey/You people). The former is also a preferred word to maintain gender neutrality.

"Folks" is gaining popularity because of its cordial tone, but it is still confusing for others.

"Macaca fuscata" macaque is Japan's national animal.

Cheery blossom is Japan's emblem, and its peak season is in March and April.

So long.

This is goodbye and not "good riddance".

Goodbye is farewell to something or someone with sadness, while good riddance is a welcome departure or loss.

I hugged her and said goodbye.

Good riddance to that manipulative colleague; she's better in retirement.

He said, "Goodbye and good riddance!" and closed the door with a slam.

Take care.

Rolade